MIND YOUR MIND

Turn Frustration into Fascination

Udaylal Pai

Copyright © 2021 Udaylal Pai

All rights reserved

The characters and events portrayed in this book are fictitious. Any similarity to real persons, living or dead, is coincidental and not intended by the author.

No part of this book may be reproduced, or stored in a retrieval system, or transmitted in any form or by any means, electronic, mechanical, photocopying, recording, or otherwise, without express written permission of the publisher.

Printed in the United States of America

Thanks!
Dr. Sahana Madhyastha Ph.D. (Psychology)

"That which moves is mind. That doesn't move is consciousness"

CONTENTS

Title Page
Copyright
Dedication
Epigraph
CHAPTER - 1   1
CHAPTER - 2   8
CHAPTER - 3   12
CHAPTER - 4   20
CHAPTER - 5   26
CHAPTER - 6   30
CHAPTER - 7   34
CHAPTER - 8   38
CHAPTER - 9   43
CHAPTER - 10   51
CHAPTER - 11   55
CHAPTER - 12   61
CHAPTER - 13   64
CHAPTER - 14   68
CHAPTER - 15   72
CHAPTER - 16   75
CHAPTER - 17   80

CHAPTER - 18	84
CHAPTER – 19	88
About The Author	103
Books By This Author	105

CHAPTER - 1

The Myth of Mind Control: If You Can't Catch the Wind, Then You Cannot Control the Mind Too

Mr.X is telling you, "A horse is standing beside you"

You look around and would say: "No - there is no horse here."

"Yes - there is one horse. You don't see doesn't mean it is not there," Mr.X talks philosophy.

You are a bit confused.

"You can see things only in three-dimension. There are fourth, fifth, and sixth dimensions. Albert Einstein and modern science have proved it…It's also mentioned in our ancient scriptures." Here Mr.X can talk about the space-time continuum and relativity theories of Einstein.

He can tell you about metaphysics, higher derivatives, and quantum mechanics other heavy subjects. Or, he can tell you how a horse can come there using futuristic technology or virtual reality, simulation, and propulsion theories that are applicable in teleportation.

If you follow any religion, he can quote something from religious texts. If you follow the Hindu religion, it is easier for him as nobody would know about their ancient scriptures. He can easily quote a couple of Sanskrit verses. And you would start believing in it.

"You can't see with naked eyes. You need inner eye," Mr.X said.

After some time, you won't be able to prove the horse is not there. At the end of the day, you are convinced that there was a horse beside you.

You couldn't see only because you are lacking something in you. You would want to fill up that void and become a higher spiritual person with enormous powers! To unleash such powers you have to concentrate, meditate and control your mind, they would say!!! And of course, there are proven methods for it, Mr.X assures you.

- This is what I told Ambika Devi, my aunt's classmate when she asked me a question: "I am not able to control my mind. I have tried many techniques like Yoga, Pranayama (breathing exercises), and Meditation. Uday, you are like my younger brother. Can you please teach me a technique to control our mind?"

"Yes, of course. Close your eyes visualize anything except a monkey..."

"I know that trick. The mind can't get rid of the image of Monkey then..." Ambika said.

"So, you know you would fail?"

"Yes...I am not able to control my Panchendriyas (five senses = sight, hearing, touch, smell, and taste).

"Aunty, you have to come out of traditional five senses. What about other Indriyas (senses)? Don't you feel Thirst, Hunger, Time, muscular Tension, etc. - are they not senses? There are at least 20 senses according to modern science - not just five senses! ..." I told her.

Even scientists aren't yet able to replicate the workings of a brain; they still don't understand the complexities and mysteries of the brain aka mind completely. The story of the mind is yet to reveal. So far, science knows the only tip of the iceberg.

And one Mr.X - a fraudster - wearing fancy dress in a cozy ambiance is telling you loud stories of mind control, and you fall for it!

Our ancestors have done extensive research for thousands of years and found the functioning of the brain and secrets of the mind. Through Upanishads, they revealed profound wisdom. But we don't have time to read it. Therefore, we can't even cross-check when Mr.X says you can control all senses or control your mind. We don't mind wasting our whole life trusting Mr.X. But we don't want to know the truth.

"Aunty, actually 99.99 percent of the people are under mind control or brain control. You are already under mind control."

"How come? I don't understand..." she said.

"Mind control is a technique used for brainwashing and re-routing the thinking process. The most powerful technique is the belief system. For instance, religions, ideologies, theologies, mafias, gangster groups, leaders, etc. can wash your brain and control your mind...When somebody questions your belief, you are getting hurt, angry, or violent, aren't you? Those are the symptoms of belief-based mind control...Not a day passes without the sad news of those brain-washed religious fanatics killing innocent people. This is mind control..."

"I know the difference between brainwashing and self-control...You are good at confusing others I know, "she has got angry and scolded me: "Here, I am talking about me controlling my mind..."

"Oh, that. But there are three issues here: One - When somebody said (or wrote) that you can control your mind, without cross-checking the credibility or source, you blindly believed it. It's like Mr.X's horse story. When I questioned your belief, you have just got angry. So, you are brainwashed. Second, you still have a kiddish immature mind which always seeks miracles and magic. Hence you accept those fairy tales of mind power as truth..."

She thought for a while and then said: "In fact, you are telling a bitter truth. Hard to accept. I really don't know if the mind can be controlled, still, I believed in it. Yes, such belief is also a brainwashed one. And the third issue is?"

"You said 'I want to control my mind' - Who is this 'I'? Obviously, it is not your body. Since you haven't realized the real self in you, your concept of "I" is actually attributed to your own mind. It is memory. It is ego. You are asking your own mind to control it. It's like entrusting the keys of your safe-locker to a thief...MIND CONTROLS YOU, Aunty. And you can't control it."

When you are born you have a clean mind with few basic commands just like the operating system in a computer. As you grow you gather inputs from surroundings (living and non-living things, parents, community, religion, teachers, etc). Those inputs are added to your system as programs and apps. Thus, your mind will have a lot of programs (apps, full-fledged operating systems, browsers, etc.) and it becomes a separate entity - a programmed robot.

As you grow, you become a slave of this programmed robot called the mind. You will then be under the command of this entity - called conditioned or robotic mind. It will put you under an auto-pilot system. (Reflect on this: You drive car thinking about the bank loans, suddenly somebody crosses the road, the autopilot in you apply sudden break).

And this robotic mind has a lot of limitations. It will work only based on the inputs or operating system that you had installed. That means your mind cannot go beyond the inputs you have received. It controls you. Mind is a control freak. You thus become just a blind slave of your mind.

The mind keeps on producing thoughts based on the programs in the brain. And as a faithful slave, all you can do is chase those thoughts. You blindly trust your thoughts. Have you ever doubted if you are thinking in the right direction? No. Why? The "I" (conditioned, robotic mind) is always right. If somebody questions the "I", you get angry.

These thoughts may make you insecure, nervous, anxious, tensed, and depressed. Your fear makes your mind more powerful day by day. It can lead you to many psychosomatic diseases. It won't let you escape from its clutches. It doesn't want any changes, except some superficial cosmetic ones. For instance, if you go for deeper meditation to change your mindset, it will cleverly coin pseudo enlightenment. You will feel that you are enlightened and will believe you are highly spiritual. The truth is your ego has inflated to the spiritual level, that's all. (For some time, it may even appear as transformed. But sooner or later your will fall back).

"I can't believe it. Everyone says Meditation is great - it will increase concentration and focus..."

"Dhyana is great. Meditation is not an apt translation for Dhyana. Dhyana is not for focusing or concentrating. Our sages said dhyana is all about awareness. It is about becoming aware that I am that - or you are that – that which is divine (Tatvamasi)."

"How to be aware?"

"Simple. By realizing you are not your mind. You are not your thoughts. You are like an infinite blue sky. Clouds come; clouds go. Sky remains. You are the Sky. Thoughts are clouds. Mind-produced thoughts will come and go. But the real me - the divine me - will remain AS IS..."

"But we may need a lot of positive thoughts to do so..."

"Positive thoughts are more harmful than negative thoughts. (Check my article on Bye-Bye Positive Thinking). When you instruct your mind to be positive, it will produce an equal and opposite amount of negative thoughts that would lead to conflicts and stress," I told her: "So, just see the thoughts the way sky sees clouds. Observe your thoughts without judgment, classification, let it come and go."

"It is not easy Uday. Thoughts would bombard in..."

"Yes, let thoughts come. Don't analyze your thoughts. Don't judge, don't control, don't justify, don't classify into good and bad...Those are just thoughts. After some time, the number of thoughts will reduce and the mind will become powerless."

"So that I can control my mind," she asked.

"There it goes again! Don't ever try to control your mind. Instead, let yourself free from the control of your mind."

"Oh"

"All you can do is managing your thoughts. The only way out is as I said, creating awareness about the property of mind, that's producing thoughts..."

"Yeah, you said it... Are there any techniques?"

"Any technique too will make you its slave. You may just sit and observe your thoughts and be aware that those are just mind-produced thoughts. You will know the limitation of your mind and will realize how the mind controls you. This awareness will lead you to your real self, which is beyond the mind. You then become aware..."

"What will happen when one is aware?"

"Once, you de-condition (being aware) yourself a realization might happen: You are not your mind. (You can think I am not my mind- but it is not realization, it is just thought.) Once the realization happens, it means you are like a virus-free laptop. You are ready for the connection..."

"Connect to what?"

"Just like a stand-alone laptop getting connected to the Internet, you can get connected to the cosmos or what they call collective consciousness. The floodgate of wisdom will open up...."

"The connection will take you to a powerful state of being?"

"What do you mean by that? I can guarantee you there won't be any magic shows, showering of flowers and fireworks. Instead, you will be lead to higher consciousness. Do any of those trillions of RBCs (red blood cells) in your blood know that it is just a small cell in your body? They are connected, right?"

"Yes, they are..."

"Those trillion cells are integral part of your body system. Similarly trillions of species, planets, stars etc are akin the cells of the whole system, which we call cosmos. You are just a species or cell in the cosmos. You're connected. The connection will make you aware that you are a cell in the organism called the cosmic. You will expand up to the universe. You will know that you are the universe, it's an integral part, you own it, and you are responsible for it. Our sages called that state Aham Brahmasmi (I am the Infinite Reality)."

"So simple and easy?"

"Yes. This awareness will prompt you to share and care for existence and life. This is the true liberation from miseries. This is eternal happiness. Aunty, don't waste your life for anything - people will take you for a bumpy ride as long as you carry such dumb and stupid concept of controlling your mind. They will just brain-wash you." I told her.

CHAPTER - 2

Really, Can't I Control My Mind?

As a matter of fact, yes, you can't!

Recently I had an opportunity to interact with a person (I can't mention his name here) who is a self-acclaimed spiritual person. He had come to meet me to introduce a new guru who is visiting our city.

He talked to me a lot of things - especially about the wrongdoing of people in what he called a materialistic world and the importance of being spiritual.

"I don't know the difference between both..." I replied.

"Ok. For, beginners like you, materialistic means being in this world. A spiritualist means he/she thinks always about the God and spiritual thing and is detached from the material comforts..."

"In that case, I am materialistic...." I said.

"These material comforts won't last much...It won't give you happiness, the cause of misery and sorrow comes from attachment to the material world" he said.

"Oh, really?" I asked.

"Yes - you have to control your mind to get a perfect happiness. That's what my guru says..."

"How do we control the mind?" I asked.

"Meditation"

"What?"

"Meditation. There are many techniques effective in controlling thoughts to get a perfect happiness. There are many methods - from focusing on objects or images, thinking through a complex idea, visualizing, chanting- all qualifying as meditation in the broad sense. Our aim is the concentration of the mind and then controlling it. Our guru teaches a new method, combining all techniques..."

"Oh, can meditation be taught? That's amusing. What's his fee?" I asked.

"Yes- that's his greatness - the initial course is absolutely free. Then you can go for an advance course for which there is only a nominal fee..."

"Oh, that is very kind of him..."

"Yes - he will teach you how to concentrate on single object/thought for long and control the mind..."

"Is it possible? I believed controlling the mind is a myth..."

"You are ignorant – with regular practice, anybody can control mind..." he said.

"Sir, you are using your own mind to control it... It is like entrusting the key to your treasury safe to a thief. The mind will keep on producing thoughts (its basic function), and you don't have any control over it. Try this today - tell your mind that you want to have a sound sleep. Most likely you won't get a night of sleep until midnight...Or try not to think about a monkey..."

"But my guru said that meditation is the concentration of the mind"

"By the way, are you talking about Dhyanam, which is wrongly translated as meditation?"

"Yes, Dhyanam. It's an Indian word. Foreigners wouldn't understand it..." he said.

"When we concentrate, there is a particular point on which we focus, and we do this to attain a particular goal. This process in itself is a tug of war. Popular belief is that meditation is a voluntary process. We sit with closed eyes in a corner of the room in a particular posture. Then we chant a particular mantra or visualize the form of a god or goddess. We may try to control our thoughts. This is what we normally call meditation. Is it right?"

"Yes - this is the method that my guru uses..."

"Sir, to my understanding, Dhyanam has nothing to do with it. Those techniques you use are only suppression of the mind, which is temporary. When the process ends the chaotic mind returns and things are back to normal... In fact, it should be the other way around, meditation should be de-concentration, just seeing the mind and observing oneself at the moment, while not resisting thoughts or emotions. It may help more. The breathing exercise (pranayama) may also help normalizing thoughts, though you can't control it"

However, many scriptures say that concentration is the first step in meditation whereas choice less awareness happens at later stages when one abandons attention. We use 'Om' to meditate which is a tool to guide our attention...So, it is okay to try concentration till he/she realizes that it wouldn't help much.

"So, how do we meditate then?"

"Meditation is not a voluntary process at all. It cannot be invited. It is not an ambitious project of an isolated mind. It happens naturally when the mind turns within itself and is aware of its own movement..."

"How would it happen?" he asked.

"Meditation happens when the petty ego of the mediator comes to an end. There is no technique to be in meditation. It happens naturally when the mind sees the limitations of all techniques and comes to an end."

"Did you have such meditation experience?"

"Sir, I have done all sort of meditation techniques only to understand its limitations. I have undergone Yoga Nidra (or yogic sleep is a state of consciousness between waking and sleeping) too. Living life in this manifested world and facing day-to-day problems in life with emotional insights itself is much more than meditation...."

"And you said you are not spiritual..."

"Sir, I do not classify anything into spiritual and material. This classification limits your mind further. My idea of happiness is that it should be limitless. I should be happy with attachments as well as in detachments. If you think you are happy only when you are detached from the material world, then your concept of happiness is limited to that. You should be happy with both of your classifications like materialism and spiritualism...because everything in the universe – both living and non-living – has a divine presence in it."

CHAPTER - 3

Meditation is Not an Item for Competition to Set Goal

"I have been meditating for one hour every day morning for the last 30 years. But I don't see any results. I have tried all techniques and methods taught by various gurus and read through a lot of books..." a reader - Sudhakar Shenoy, 47 years, Pune - told me.

He asked me: "How was your meditating experience Udaymam?" (Mam is often used as equivalent to Shri or Mister in Konkani language)

"You mean to ask, did I hear the bell ringing? Did I smell fragrance? Or did the heaven shower flowers?" I smiled at him.

"Yes, something like that...meditation is a divine journey of the soul from Muladhara (the root center of spiritual power in the human body, as per Hindu Tantrism) to Sahasrarapadma (the crown center which is known as "the bridge to the cosmos), right? That's what a Guru (he mentioned the name of a famous Swami) taught me. But I didn't experience anything. I don't think I can reach the Samadhi (the highest state of total self-collectedness). My Guru said that's because of my fault and past sins...Is it so?"

"I also have read about such things, but I don't know for sure. You better ask your learned Gurus. My understanding of Dhyana (meditation is a loose translation of Dhyanam, but let me use it) is different."

"What technique do you use for meditation, Udaymam?" he

asked.

Techniques and tools are particularly important for him, as he was conditioned in that way. "I am very much confused. Many Gurus talk about various meditation methods," he said.

"For me, meditation is not a skill or academic subject to learn from any Gurus. A Guru can teach his perception or concepts of meditation...If that suits you, you can follow it...But I began meditation with a rational mind as I had a healthy disrespect to all Gurus and all related scriptures..."

"What is the technique that you used...?"

"Shenoy maam, for ease let me use the word Meditation for Dhyana, which happens naturally when our mind sees the limitations of all techniques, tools, methods, or guidelines...any tool or technique will make you slave of it. You will remain addicted to it. It can't help you to cross over, liberate or realize. Meditation, as I see, is de-conditioning and conscious awakening from a state of sleep."

"What do you mean by sleep? How to wake up?"

"It is just waking up. When you wake up from sleep (concepts, perspective, conditioning) you become aware of the divinity within you. You will know you're a perfect person with all your imperfections."

"Ok...I can understand it on a conceptual level...but how did you reach there?"

"I can share with you only my experience. You may have a different one. I began with rational thinking. I have read, listened, and learned many things. But intellectual knowledge didn't help me with emotional insights. I understood that knowledge as information won't transform me. The intellectual or logical understanding won't liberate me. Rationalism helps me up to the mind level of achievements. The knowledge I acquire just adds up to my ego only. An egoistic mind controls me. I found that my mind is deeply conditioned that cannot see anything objectively. I realized that I have to address my mind first..."

"Is that why you started meditating?" he jumped in between, "But how did you concentrate your mind? How did you control it?" Sudhakar Shenoy was getting impatient.

"Those who propagate meditation as a "concentrating mind" believe that meditation is a voluntary process. We sit with closed eyes in a corner of the room (in places of worship or Ashrams) in a particular assigned posture or Yoga posture. Then we chant any mantra or sacred stanza from Holy Books or visualize the form of a God or Goddess. We may then try to control our thoughts, this is what they say. This is what you normally call meditation, right?"

"Yes, what else?"

"I know that's the popular misconception and perception. But it didn't work for me. As per my humble experience, meditation is de-concentration. For me, it is not possible to concentrate on a single object/thought/chant for long..."

"That's true. I had also experienced. It is not possible to control the mind..."

"Mind controls you. You can't control your mind. To this day, except in folklore or myth, nobody has ever controlled his/her mind. The gist of our Upanishads teaching, to my understanding, is a one-liner: That which moves is mind. That doesn't move is GOD"

"Beautiful...that's true. Mind moves. But everybody talks about concentrating/focusing mind..."

"Concentration or control of the mind is only temporary suppression of the thoughts or mind. When the process or technique ends the chaotic mind returns and things are back to normal...."

"Did you have any specific place for meditation? Prayer room? Place of solitude?"

"I feel meditation should be done only in a busy and noisy place, like market, cinema theatre and in a train or bus. If I go and meditate in the Himalayas, Ashrams, or Temples, what will I do when I come back? I am living my life here, not in solitude. My problems are here, not there."

"So how did you meditate?"

"Meditation is not a voluntary process. It cannot be invited. It is not the determined project of an isolated mind. It happens naturally when we look within and become aware of the mind's own movement. When I looked within me, I saw the conditioning, the depth of my desire and ego. I saw how those thoughts manipulate me."

"So, what technique did you use?"

"You are still chasing techniques. Meditation happens naturally when you see the limitations of all techniques. There is no goal, no time frame, and no struggle. It should be effortless. It's all about being aware of oneself."

"I understand - how did you do that?"

"Just sit comfortably. Any posture. Observing your thoughts would lead to awareness. There is no process at all..."

"Yes, but how did you observe your thoughts?"

"I began with listening to various sounds around me. Initially, it was disturbing. But I cannot stop others from making sounds. So, I just listened to that without fighting it, then I found there is a silence in between the sounds. I felt at peace with sounds. Then I began observing my mind - that's my thoughts. Not fighting the thoughts. Just observed it without judging or analyzing it. I stopped classifying thoughts into good and bad. Thus, I stopped getting involved with those thoughts..."

"Then what happened?" he was very eager to know.

"As I observed I found that I am not my thoughts. Till then, I was stupid to follow my thoughts. I had believed that all my thoughts to be true. Whatever thoughts coming to me is right, I thoughts..."

As we discussed earlier, we cannot completely rule out the role of concentrated ways of meditating which would have worked for few people. However, concentration or paying attention can be a tool for a good beginning.

"So, thoughts are not true..."

"Thoughts are just a product of a conditioned mind. So, it can't be true or objective. Thoughts come, thoughts go, but I remain. I became aware that there is a gap between one thought and the next one. While I was consciously waiting for the next thought, it refused to come. That gap of thoughtless state slowly widened. I became aware of my thoughts, emotions, and actions...Slowly, I became just a witness of my thoughts and I stopped chasing thoughts...I felt at peace. Thoughts stopped troubling me. I am aware."

"Then what would be the final thing?"

"Nothing...mediation is not a competition item or game or event to set a goal. Please don't set any goals. Just be aware. By being aware, you will become aware of your life and love and the connection with the divinity."

"What change occurred to you? Have you become steady?"

"The change was mostly internal. Externally I am all the same. I found the sum reasons for all my problems. I am my problem, nothing else. I was responsible for everything. I = my ego. I understood that there is two type of ego - direct (ahankara) and subtle (fear). Both types of ego surface because I think I am separate. As long as I feel separate from existence, I will have both types of ego. The awareness led me to connectedness. When I experienced that I am not alone in this cosmos and I am not separate from the cosmos, the ego dissolved..."

"Can you explain "connectedness" Udaymam?"

"It is simple - a water drop jumps up from a wave in the ocean and says 'I am a separate individual. My name is water drop' - that's separation, that's ego. The water drop has a life span of less than a second. Then it falls down and dissolves into the ocean. A man has a life span of fewer than 100 years (when compared to the Earth or cosmos, this is a minuscule unit). Just like the water drop we also think we are separate from the cosmos. This thought of separation creates ego, which will remain till we die and dissolve in the system called cosmos. If you meditate and be aware, you will become aware of that connectedness. That's when you are awakened. That's my understanding of Dhyanam..."

"Still confused with the connectedness...The water drop is connected to the ocean. But what about us?"

"What's that in your finger and around the neck?"

"My wedding ring and my chain..."

"I would say both are gold. Chain and ring are names or forms. But the content is gold. Gold is the real thing..."

"Yes, I also know it is gold. But how is it related to meditation and connectedness?"

"The water drop understood that it was the ocean. Water drop is the name and form. Ring and chain are names and forms of the same gold. Sudhakar Shenoy is a name and form. Udaylal Pai is also just a name and form. But the content that we are made up of is the same which is known as cosmos - the totality (In Sanskrit, it is called Brahmam)"

"So that's the result of meditation?"

"It is not a result. It just naturally happens to everybody who is aware. When you realize you are made up of Brahmam, what would be the next natural move? You will want to know what that Brahmam is. The end of meditation is the beginning of something known as "athato brahma jijnasa..." I said.

"What does that mean?"

"Hmm...'athato brahma jijnasa' the first aphorism in the Vedanta-sutra (Brahma Sutra). That means: 'now, therefore, one should inquire about Brahmam". or "Now is the time to inquire about the Absolute Truth". No Guru, nothing, can take you to that stage. You have to go on your own. It's not just searching."

"Then?"

"The seeker and the process of seeking and the sought - all become one. What will happen to a salt doll which goes to measure the depth of the ocean? It will get dissolved and become one with the ocean, right? Similarly, this inquiry has to be experienced. The ego (the feeling of 'I') will be dissolved in that Source. There is then NO 'I' and 'You' to tell stories or teach others. So how can anybody teach you this? It cannot be described or explained. It cannot be taught. Every human being is programmed to reach there - some choose that, some don't. That's all" I said.

"Have you experienced it?"

"No. I stopped at 'Athato brahma jijnasa'. I am happy and contented with what I have. I have some karma to do. So, I decided to inquire after some time." I smiled at him.

"Udaymam, I didn't know it was that simple..." he paused for a while and said: "I have wasted my time with fancily-dressed swamis and gurus... huh...You are right! You are absolutely right..."

"You are making the same mistake. How do you know I am right? You are jumping to a conclusion without verifying or experiencing what I said. You still expect others to throw light unto your inner self. It cannot be provided by others. And I don't think all Swamis and Gurus are wrong. They are just telling you their perception earnestly."

"Udaymam, you have spent a lot of your valuable time and energy for an unknown person like me, that too without expecting or accepting anything in return. So how can you be wrong?"

"Shenoymam, I am a small writer. I am sharing whatever I learned or experienced - that's my humble Manav Seva(service towards humanity). Every human being is a unique expression. My experiences can be wrong for you. So please do it for yourself and don't blindly follow anybody. It's something between you and your source. When the source is readily available for you why should you go to middlemen to learn meditation?"

CHAPTER - 4

Does the Human Mind Possess Any "Superpowers"?

Some people have keen eyesight, some don't. Some people have acute hearing, some don't.

Similarly, for some, the performance of the brain (yes, mind) is better and sharper than others. Just like eyes and ears, the brain is also an organ. It doesn't have any extra power that other people do not have.

You might have read a lot about "Mind Power" - the miraculous and amazing power of your mind. There are a lot of stories and incidents about the phenomena called - mind over matter.

"I have read that if you concentrate and focus your mind, you can perform many fantastic things - miracles," messaged a reader.

"Really? Why do you want to live in fool's paradise?"

Let's analyze the facts and truths.

Let's make it simple. I know you have a stand-alone personal computer, laptop, tablet, or at least a mobile handset. Every device has two segments - hardware and software. The basic hardware consists of the processor, hard disk (storage), memory, and wiring. The software part consists of an operating system and programs in it. The power of the device depends upon the speed of the processor and the size of the memory and storage. Of course, it needs energy (electricity) to operate.

Any stand-alone device has very limited capacity or power within a stipulated, predefined system. But when it gets connected to the Internet (wired or wireless) - you can unleash its unlimited powers. You can do zillions of things using the same device.

Our mind (aka brain) is similar to such a device. The brain is a bundle of hardware plus software (chemical processes).

Our ancestors called it (brain, mind, and process together) Antahkaranams. According to them, the system is divided into four: Manas (Mind), Buddhi (Intelligence), Chittam (Memory), and Ahankara (Egoism).

Before going deep into that, let's see the limitations of the stand-alone mind

The mind can NEVER survive in the intense present. For instance, when "wow" happens to you, you forget the mind. You're in the no-mind situation when such extreme happiness occurs.

The mind thrives on the past and future. The moment you come to a status of 'HERE and NOW', the mind ceases to exist.

Similarly, the mind cannot comprehend the absolute or abstract truth. It needs facts, figures, and images. Any belief is Okay with the mind, but NO truth, please. The mind cannot KNOW anything beyond the senses that you have. Mind itself can be called sixth sense, but it cannot understand that.

The stand-alone mind cannot experience the cosmos or its divine presence. Take for instance, what happens when people call that divine existence of the cosmos God. The mind can understand the concepts, perception, or belief about God. But it can never experience the existence of GOD. Therefore, the mind has no powers of its own as fantasized by the fiction writers.

The mind survives only with the ego. Ego means the feeling of "I" or the memory of "I". This ego makes the stand-alone mind insecure. So, it always seeks psychological security. That's why we clinch to so many beliefs, faiths, and superstitions. We are comfortable with such beliefs and when we face harsh truths of life, we clinch upon such beliefs, and not the reality.

Now about the hardware part of the mind. The hardware is the content of the mind or the material that the mind is made up of. "Is Mind a material? It has physical form?" You might ask. Yes, it has.

Our ancient scientists (that is Hindu ancestors, the sages) say it is material. Incidentally, our ancestors used the Mantra Sakthi (Sankalp - through deep Dhyanam) to discover many things in humans and the cosmos. Western science use Yantra Sakthi (machines, types of equipment, computers, etc).

Through the Mantra Sakthi, the ancients could view what is – that is in Sankalp (a sort of seeing virtual reality through factual imagination). The dhyana and samadhi (enlightenment etc) might have helped them.

In the Brihadaranyaka Upanishad, the mind is looked upon as material. The Chandogya Upanishad says" anna mayam hi somya mana "means "The mind is verily composed of food." Food is churned inside by the energies of our body and takes three different forms: the heaviest becomes excrement, the medium quality becomes flesh, and the subtlest part becomes mind, just as the churning of curds gives the subtlest which is butter.

The Upanishad explains how they conducted the research that we can repeat in modern times too. It mentions an experiment in which a boy was asked to go on fast for 15 days. "Do not eat any food for fifteen days. Just drink water." On the fifteenth day, the boy was asked to recite the Vedas that he memorized. "I cannot remember even one verse of the Vedas. Memory has gone. The mind is not functioning." The boy said.

Your mind has been inflamed into action by the food that you have taken. Your mind would perish if you had not eaten well. So the content of the mind is made up of the food you eat. You cannot see, feel or taste your mind - it is subtle material and not gross like your body.

Let's look at the software part of the mind. When we are born, our mind has a biological operating system (BIOS) which has some basic minimum commands - like crying, sucking mother's breast milk, etc. Later, we add inputs to it - from parents, relatives, friends, teachers, community, religions, beliefs, reading, learning, etc. Those inputs altogether form a huge operating system along with programs fed by your belief system.

That's how the mind is been developed. No wonder, many learned people said that God created everything, except your mind. Mind is your creation. And that's is the limit of the mind.

A game developed for Windows operating system cannot run in Apple iMac. Similarly, things beyond your inputs have no compatibility with your mind. Your mind cannot understand anything that is not in the inputs.

The fully loaded (pre-loaded software) mind is known as CONDITIONED MIND. If you have a malicious infection (virus or malware) the mind will go wrong. That creates negative emotional states such as anger, stress anxiety, and sadness. In some cases, one can get exposed to diseases such as depressions and schizophrenia. However, according to science, there are other reasons too.

When you realize these basic facts, you will know that all those tall stories related to the power of the mind are cinematic or dramatic fiction.

"Then, how did our ancestors used the Mantra Sakthi?"

Good question. The connected mind is powerful and divine: -

Our ancestors were connected to the cosmic system which otherwise is called collective consciousness. The cosmic wisdom stored in the universe (the collective consciousness) is like the data center in cloud computing. Dhyana (meditation is not the apt translation) provided the wireless connection to the servers in the data center.

How to make your mind powerful?

1. Check-up hardware part - Sattvik food (seasonal and fresh foods) will make your hardware strong and powerful.

Provide two plates of food to a modern teenager. On one plate keep typical traditional South Indian Idly Sambar and on another plate keep a Chicken Burger. What would he/she prefer - irrespective of caste and religion? Of course, Burger!

In my childhood, I remember the old generation was reciting "Vishnusahasranamam" and "Lalitha Sahasranamam" by-heart. Most of them kept everything in their memory. In today's world, memory is short term affair. Why? You may attribute this to hi-fi gadget use of which does not require any brain memory. Ancients did their math by using a brain, now you have a calculator, so you don't have to do it byheart. But truth is that the older generations were having "sattvic" food and the modern generation goes by fast food. According to the older generation, "fast food = short-term memory"...I don't have any scientific proof for that.

Food is important for the brain and mind. Based on these concepts our Ayurveda scholars developed some medicines (Grita - is ghee medicated with ayurvedic herbs and kashaya) that cross the blood–brain barrier (BBB) that can change the mindset. That's how they rectified mental diseases in the olden days.

2. Check-up software part - The only way to cross over the limitations of the mind is to de-condition it. Run an anti-virus program. It is freely available. It is known as Awareness. It can be achieved only through observing.

3. Get connected to the cosmic network - Use the "I" as a login name. Password is deleting the "I". Once you log on to the Net, you don't even need the password. You are IN. The vastness of the cosmic is waiting for you. You will be aware of the truth that you're an integral part of the cosmos. This connectedness will make you strong and powerful. You won't have any fear of the

stand-alone mind. Because you are connected to GOD. You become God. Ancient called this awareness "Aham Brahmasmi" (individual self-integrates to the Absolute).

Ancients knew that a standalone mind is dangerously weak. They knew that the separation causes ego and fear. Once you are connected, you become fearless. You become one with the vastness. It has programs to correct your system and any aberrations of the mind.

We are all human; we all share the same range of emotions we are capable of feeling. What makes us different is how we react to these emotions. Nobody can perform any power that you cannot.

Miracles of mind or amazing powers are just magic. It is not the true way. If you are attracted to the miracle of the mind, you won't learn the true way. The biggest power or miracle is about becoming more fully human. It is the end of ignorance. That's why the greatest Zen master once said: "My miracle is that when I'm hungry, I eat, and when I am tired, I sleep."

CHAPTER - 5

A Depressed Girl and The Butterfly Effect

Recently I met Rajani (not real name) during a wedding ceremony. She said she was a regular reader of my articles on the website. We talked for some time.

She is doing her post-doctoral research. Her husband is a highly paid medical doctor. He is having an affair with another woman (his fellow worker). He drinks heavily. And whenever possible he harasses her talking about her past love affair. She is not getting support from her parents too. Her brother has cheated on her for acquiring the family property. "I would want to go for a job to avoid the mental torture. But that would be an end to my research. So many years of hard work would go to waste. I am in a confused state of mind..."

The helplessness, no-hope situation, stress, frustration, etc., have put her down. She is on medication for depression. She has insomnia and some physical ailments too. "I am feeling very lonely. My life is wasted and worthless. Sometimes I get thoughts about committing suicide. I am really scared about such thoughts too." She appeared timid and tense.

"Do you know about the butterfly effect?" I asked her.

"No"

"It has been said that something as small as the flutter of a butterfly's wings can ultimately cause a typhoon halfway around the world. A butterfly flapping its wings in one part of the world might ultimately cause a hurricane in another part of the world. E.g., a butterfly flapping its wings in the Amazon jungle might create a Tsunami in Indonesia"

"Oh, really?"

"Tell me, how many cells are there in a human body?"

It was her subject of study. She said: "At maturity, the estimated number of cells in the body is given as 37.2 trillion. Some calculations say that for an adult man weighing 70 kilograms has 70 trillion cells."

"However, it is in trillions! And if one cell doesn't do its work (karma) properly, what will happen?"

"Hmmm...Illness. If a cell multiplies more than required, it can cause tumor (malignant or not) or if cells start dying before time, it may end up in cancer..."

"Does the cell know that it is part of a system called the human body and is connected to trillions of cells?"

"No...how can it be? It doesn't have such intelligence. It does its duty, that's all" she said.

"Yes, it doesn't know its purpose of life. But, it does its duty or karma properly, hence the human body is well-maintained. We call it a healthy body."

"Right"

"Now tell me, what is the population of the world?" I asked her.

"According to 2012 figures, the population of the world = 7.046 billion"

"Rajani, the whole world is a system like the human body. We do not realize that we are part of the system. We do not realize that we are all connected. If one person among 700 crores does not do his/her karma properly, the entire system will be affected. One cell can harm the whole body. One human being can create chaos in the system. And one planet can create havoc in the galaxy. The entire universe is sustaining in a delicate balance by the virtue of the law of attraction, which is known as love. If the fluttering of a butterfly can create such widespread destruction, what a human being is capable of?"

"Hmmm. Unbelievable, but logical..."

"Our ancestors knew this - That's why they prayed "Loka Samastha Sukhino Bhavantu" (May all beings everywhere be happy). They considered the entire world as "Vasudhaiva Kutumbakam" (The world is my family). Just like any creatures in this world, every human being has karma. We have to do our karma. If you try to evade your karma, that's adharma (non-virtuous). If your husband is not doing his karma properly, he should be worried about that, not you...He will get the result of his karma..."

"Really?" I could see the change in her mind through her eyes.

"Rajani, you may feel lonely. But you are not alone. The entire universe is there for you - as your own. The separation is ego. The feeling of separation creates loneliness, fear, and selfishness. The moment you realize the connectedness, you would feel happy and enlightened..."

"But what about these problems I face, Uday?"

"Rajani, every problematic situation in life is a cosmic invitation to become better. Being sattvic in food habits and thoughts would solve 90 percent of the problems."

"What would I do now?"

"You are an intelligent researcher. Your findings would be of great use to the entire humanity. Not everybody can do the things that you do. Why does this situation appear in your life? It shows you have a purpose. Most human beings do their karma, without knowing their real purpose in life. (Just like cells in the human body). They are auto-piloted by the conditioned mind and never try to cross over or wake up. The existence provides situations in life to wake you up from the conditioning. Make use of it and live a life with awareness. You are supposed to do this research. You have to focus on your karma, come what the result may be. I can see things will turn to be good."

"Will things be better for me?"

"Yes - things will be good for you, not your good, but the good's good..."

A smile came to her face: "Oh, is there a good's good too? Truly?"

"Even for the truth, there have been three versions. Your truth, his truth, and truth's truth" I said.

She laughed: "You could have taken up the profession of a counselor"

"But, my karma is writing. I am aware of it. I am supposed to touch only a few people's lives like that of yours who are destined to meet me..."I said.

"Yes Uday, I will focus on my karma..." she appeared more cheerful.

CHAPTER - 6

Turn Frustration to Fascination

"Dear Uday, I have been reading all your articles in your website. I have been living in US for the last 45 years with my children and grand kids. I do meditation, prayers, rituals, read all puranas etc. I am very spiritual and strict vegetarian. Still, I am frustrated and depressed. I am suffering from some diseases too. I want to talk to you - please send me your phone number if you actually 'care and share' (Or is it just caption of your site?)?" This was the gist of a letter from Mrs. Nandini Raman.

I replied to her: "Relax. But who told you that you won't get disease if you follow all those things? " I gave her my contact details asking her to fix a mutually convenient time to talk.

She called me next day. She is feeling sort of alienated. Her husband passed away. Children have grown up and settled nearby. Grand-children are almost Americans. She is frustrated. "I have read your articles many times. You always talk about the real and manifested self. And you said if we realize the real self we would be happy."

"That's right..."

"It's easier said than done. How do we practice it in life?"

"What's your favorite TV program?" I asked.

"What?"

I repeated the question. Then she said: "I get 'Devon Ke Dev... Mahadev' (a Hindi television program, I guess) here in New York"

"You are seeing it in your TV LED screen, right?"

"Yes"

"Yes - you are seeing the program on the plain LED screen. When you watch the program, the LED screen doesn't disappear. You don't notice the screen as you are involved in watching the program. The forget about the display screen. But it is very much there. You overlooked the screen because of your fascination of the program..."

"Yes..."

"You lost sight of screen as you are getting attracted to the program. Good. Can you recognise the screen during the program? No. You are aware that program is just an illusion on the screen; still, you won't recognize the screen."

"How can you compare it with my life?"

"There is a real you - you may call it in many names like "the real self, being or existence or divine", whatever. And there is a manifested You that includes your mind and body. Your manifested self feels the world is real. And it always searches for the missing things like happiness. It is not lost to be found"

"Hmm..."

"The real you (LED screen) has been overlooked because of the fascination and identification with the manifested self (mind and body). The manifested you is in fact a conditioned program. When you watch an interesting movie in the TV Screen, you would become tensed, happy, thrilled, and angry, sometimes shout, laugh aloud, cry...right? The movie lasts for maximum 1 or 2 hours. The manifested you (a program) may last for 70-80 years..."

"But how can you compare 1 or 2 hours to a human life expectancy of 70 years?" she asked.

"Compare your life expectancy with that of earth which is billions of years. The life expectancy of a galaxy is trillions of years. The real you is eternal. It doesn't die - it just changes forms. So the real you doesn't have insecurity or fear. It is just happy..."

"How can we find the real self?"

"You have to find your path. You may try to minus the mind and body from you…"

"Any clues like they give in TV shows?"

"Being aware may help you. I can't say for sure. I can share with you my experience. I was anxious and fearful. I wanted to be happy. I wanted more. I wanted to change the situation…."

"Yeah - yeah - same issue here…"

"I couldn't change much. So, I asked myself: "Who is this "I" that wants to be happy? Who is that always "wants" something? I asked myself. What are you? I want to know you. I want to see you. I want to get acquainted with you…"

"But difficult to practice…"

"It is easy. The real "I" doesn't want anything - it always is happy and contented. For, it knows, the entire universe belongs to it. But the manifested "I" (the program) wants many things. In body level, it wants comforts, pleasure and easiness. In the mind level, it wants happiness and peace. It is insecure, as it is separated from the real "I". The insecurity creates fear."

"Yeah, I know that. But how can I overcome the current situation"?She sounded better.

"The current (or any given) situation is either provided by god or is the result of your Karma. If it is provided by god, leave it to god. God knows better. If it is the result of your karma, nobody else is responsible for the situation. In both cases, there is no point in wasting time on worrying about it."

"Hmm..."

"So, as the first step, accept the situation as is! It is your interpretation and analysis that makes the situation bad to worse. It is just a situation that happens in the program known as "manifested you". The "real you" or the LED screen is still intact without any change."

"It sounds easy now. But after some time, all those thoughts would come, over power me. No philosophy works then..."

"Madam, you may go according to your fascination, but be grounded on the real "I". In your favorite program, even if a sad scene comes up, your fascination to the program won't be reduced. So, get fascinated by the program as is. Your role is already assigned in the program. Act well. Just engross in acting that let all think it is for real. In fact, living truthfully under the imaginary circumstances is your role in life. Do it earnestly...."

"You mean to say engross myself in the drama called life?"

"Yes –but check every moment: " am I grounded in the real I?" Live a life with the realization that you are actually the LED Screen and not the program. So, every moment of your life, you would be happy and contented. And you will know, the program will get over after some time, but the screen will remain!"

CHAPTER - 7

Mind Your Mind

"Sir...please help me, I am totally stressed out. I can't bear this tension...I am getting panic attacks...." A call around 1.30 AM yesterday. I am a poor sleeper who had been sleeping for 3-4 hours a day for the last 30 years! Recently I enjoy luxury of sleeping for around 5 hours a day. This call from UAE was really irritating as I lost my precious sleep.

"Brother, you need help of a psychiatrist or psychologist. I am just not that...." I said.

"No Sir, I have read your articles like 'Chat with film star', 'Do you feel insecure?' and 'Bye-bye positive thinking'...I was getting solace from them...I am very much obliged to you sir..."

"Oh, that's why you called me at this time in the night?"

He didn't understand the annoyance in my reply. "Yes, sir..." he replied earnestly.

"Mathew (not real name), there is a sign board near my house showing direction to MG Road. We have to see the direction and go to destination. The sign board won't go...I am just a writer. I write about my experiences in life...If you read it and get something useful from it, that's well and good for you. But I haven't and won't give any paid service to bother me like this," I said very curtly.

"Sir- you are the only person I can depend on now...You said you would be available for those who seek..."

"Yes- in my free time only..." I make sure that I reply to each and every letter and message that I get everyday - I spend nearly two hours a day for that. I spend more time on somebody, only if I feel it intuitively. Otherwise, I have my other karma too. "I clearly said that you've to message me first and fix up mutually convenient time..."

"Sir - please...it is regarding my family..." he went on explaining. It is a bit complicated story - but the issue is that at present he is so tensed and experiencing extreme anxiety.

I became normal. I already have lost my sleep. He is a computer guy. He needs help from a psychologist or probably prescription for medicine from a psychiatrist right now. He is not willing to meet them...The only thing I can try doing is some sort of deviation technique.

"OK Mathew, where are you now?"

"I am outside the flat Sir, in the garden..."

"Ok, keep the phone down somewhere, close your eyes and walk. Count up to 500..."I said.

He called me after few minutes: "Sir..."

"What happened?"

"Sir, I hit in many places, fell down twice and my right feet thumb has got hurt..." I understood that he was a bit relieved from his tension as his focus was deviated.

"That means if you close your eyes, you are not able to walk properly...."

"Right"

"Leg is just a body organ"

"Yes..."

"So is your brain...Please understand YOUR BRAIN IS JUST AN ORGAN...You have a laptop, right?"

"Yes"

"Just like the software programs loaded in the laptop, your brain is filled with various programs that entered as inputs from your childhood. Your brain is conditioned with those inputs or programs. Mind is the operating system (OS) of the brain. Mind is also a thought producing factory. It produces files and files of thoughts... Why should you trust thoughts coming from such a conditioned brain?"

"Sir?"

"I said mind or brain is just another organ that produces thoughts. Your leg is a body organ used for walking. But with closed eyes you couldn't walk. You need eyes to see...Similarly, if you don't see your thoughts properly, it will create hurts, hits and falls."

"How to see it?"

"DON'T TRUST YOUR THOUGHTS. Those are just thoughts produced by a thought producing organ called your conditioned brain. Your laptop needs wireless connectivity with an Internet Service Provider (ISP) to get real on time Google map, right? Similarly, to see your thoughts properly, your brain needs to get connected."

"Which ISP sir?"

I laughed hearing that innocent question. "Here the ISP is known as collective consciousness or cosmic energy or divine power or Gods, whatever - whichever - an ISP that gives you such a free Wi-FI service..."

"How to do it sir?" his sounded more enthusiastic and better.

"There is a Wireless Networking Software in you. That's known as 'surrendering program'. Leave everything to God. God has better wisdom than your rubbish brain. Don't trust your thoughts. Especially, when you are anxious, don't trust the poor logic presented by baseless thoughts from your disturbed brain..."

I told him to pray to his God's mother (he believes in Jesus Christ), leave things to her and go to sleep. Everything will be alright, I said. What else can I do? However, today morning he called me again to say thanks - it seems that trick worked! He said he was relaxed and went to bed with almost calm mind.

I got the idea of surrender to the feet of God's mother from the following phrase:

"Aapathim kim karaneeyam?" (What will you do in a clear and present danger?)

"Smaraneeyam charanayugalamambaya" (Think about Goddess Durga's (Mothers) feet)

When people like Mathew call me, sometimes I advise them to recite a moola mantra (any mantra that comes to my mind that time) depending upon the situation - and to my surprise, it works in 99% cases. There is no scientific proof for the power of mantra. But there is no scientific proof for the existence of God too!

However, this was a lesson for me too. I switch off mobile phone at 9PM and stopped providing my personal number. Instead, anyone can reach me through text in my WhatsApp number and fix up mutually convenient time.

CHAPTER - 8

*Caution: Positive Thinking
May Be Harmful to You*

Does Positive Thinking Work All the time? Is it a pseudo-scientific con?

Promod is an MLM (multi-level-marketing) businessman. He also runs a business of personality development. He told me: "Positive thinking has miraculous powers. Positive thinkers are successful in life. It is a proven fact. I am a positive thinker. I read a lot about the power of positive thinking. Everyday morning and before going to bed I make auto-suggestions on positive attitude."

I asked him: "What's your goal in life?"

"My first aim is to buy a waterfront bungalow - I am positive about it..."

"So, you are not happy now, but you will be happy in the future when you buy the bungalow. Hence you are trying your level best with a positive mindset"

"Yes..."

"The more you are affirming that you would be happy when you get a Bungalow, an equal and opposite quantity of thoughts are being produced in your subconscious, saying that you are not happy now. That means, in the current given situation you are unhappy..."

"Yes- I am unhappy, that's why I am striving to reach my goal..."

"This tells your state of mind. If you are not happy now with what you have, you will never be happy. The unhappy Promod is moving forward, not a happy Promod. So, even if you reach the destination, only the unhappy Promod will be reaching the goal."

"What do you mean?" he asked.

"If you need full energy to work towards your goal, you should be happy and contented right now. You have to work towards your goal with a happy mind. A happy mood produces happy hormones in the body. It's a scientific fact. Positive thinking will indirectly create toxic thoughts which will be suppressed in the subconscious. Being happy is more important because it is your energy which has to match that of your source (higher self, the God-given flow of energy, or whatever you prefer to call)."

"How can you say that positive thinking will indirectly create toxic thoughts?"

"There lies an inherent stream of negative thinking deep beneath the sheen of positive thinking. The mind picks it up to produce toxic thoughts. Over-doze of positive thinking is harmful too. Whenever we use affirmations like "I can do it", the "I", the underlying self (ego) develops resistance. This resistance and negative thoughts are then pushed into the unconscious. The reality of life is that the unconscious directs behaviors and we are more unconscious than conscious. Positive thinking can create unrealistic expectations that may lead to depression, especially when one does not achieve them in the planned period of time. You will be exhausted by the effort of trying to think positively always. You'll be fed up with the hype surrounding "positive thinking". Many people say that positive thinking is so superficial that it's depressing"

"You mean it is bad to think positive?"

"Positive thinking can have some psychological relevance, but no existential relevance whatsoever. For people with minor problems such as temporary setbacks, it could be helpful. But people who think they can use positive thinking to get out of depression or counter addiction are setting themselves up for failure. Positive thinking can disguise real mental health problems. It can have devastating results for many people. For most people, these deliberate attempts to think positively often compromise their well-being in the future."

"So, we should work without positive thinking? What a ridiculous argument?"

"I am not arguing with you. You are succumbing to positive thinking because you do not know how to be happy now and you can't handle reality. You want to skip the negative and just think positive."

"But positive thinking people are successful," Promod said.

This is a popular misconception and belief. It is the most harmful marketing strategy that the US managers were promoting all over the world. Positive thinking is an American phenomenon. It is still promoted as one of the keys to success and happiness, though science has proven otherwise.

"All successful people are not positive thinkers. Some just became successful because they landed on the right idea at right time and it took off and made them money. I know many, many people are struggling in debt - ordinary people. Will a positive frame of mind help them to overcome that? You think that you're not going to get sick, your vehicle is not going to break down, and you're not going to lose your job…Will positive thinking help here?"

"Are you a negative thinker?"

"No. But I feel that negative thinking gives you more experience by accepting the fact that something that happened was wrong and that it has to change for the better. I found that most depressed or pessimistic people have a more accurate view of themselves and their environment. So it isn't negative to be totally and bluntly honest with yourself and see things as they really are instead of sugar-coating the truth with positivity. Positivity is good for sales and con games, nothing more."

"So, you are not a positive thinker, not a negative thinker so what do you hope for?"

"Instead of optimism or pessimism, what about trying pragmatic realism? Or transcendental thinking? Or logical thinking?" I asked.

"So, you mean to say that I should be happy now, and work towards my goal without positive or negative thinking?

"Yes - If you are currently happy, when you reach the goal, the happiness will increase. And in the unfortunate event of not reaching the goal, (because you are already happy) you will not be depressed. You have done your level best; though you couldn't achieve it. Thus, the mind will find solace…"

"So, we have to work with a happy mood?"

"Yes – you have set a goal -it may be a want, desire, or need whatever. The struggle of working towards the goal should make you happier. So, you will be dedicated and determined in doing the work (karma), not in the result. You always derive happiness in working towards the goal. Then if you reach the goal, you will feel really great, but not an egotist. If you don't reach the goal, ok, that's sad indeed, but you won't be heartbroken or depressed, because you are already happy and you have enjoyed every moment till then. So, your calm and relaxed mind would think of another alternative or plan-B."

I don't know if he followed that. But it remains a fact that what you try to avoid becomes the basis of your consciousness. So be careful!

CHAPTER - 9

The Ancient 'Stress Buster' Formula

Stress and anxiety, worries, panic attacks, depression, bipolar disorders, obsessive-compulsive disorder, phobias, personality disorders, mood disorders, general fears, and mood swings... the list of mental disorders and other mental conflicts are on a perpetual rise...

"My son has some mental problems. "Is it a curse?"

"I have some mental issues, is it because of sin?"

"Is it caused by evil influence?"

"Is it an attack by negative energy?"

"Is it demonic possession?"

"Has somebody done black magic to ruin me?"

"Is it owing to evil planets?"

"Are Gods angry with me?"

"It appears somebody has put an evil 'eye' on my family"... I used to get all such questions. It may appear non-sense to modern man, but for the sufferer it is real. The sufferer would believe in anything when in trouble.

Fortunately, the sages who created Vedic scriptures, our ancestors, were NOT as superstitious as modern men! So, if you really want a mentally healthy progeny, listen to them.

The ancients have well-researched about the human mind rationally and developed a perfect lifestyle to maintain a healthy mind even for future generations.

They classified stress (or any other mental disorders) into two groups: (1) Naisargika (Natural or inborn) and (2) Arjita (earned, acquired, or obtained).

"Naisargika" (Natural) is further sub-divided into four – Atmajam (born or descended or caused by the immaterial and immortal part of a human being or animal), Mathrujam (born or descended or caused by mother), Pithrujam (born or descended or caused by Father) and Vargajam (born or descended or caused by race).

According to ancients, some mental diseases are derived from previous (past) lives which are carried by Jeevatma (the individual self). It is related to unidentified memories. It's a vast subject, I cannot explain this in a small space now, hence skipping this part for now.

In the modern world, Pithrujam, Mathrujam, and Vargajam can be combined into one – genetic or DNA related.

The modern world has no remedy or solution for 'Naisargika' mental disorders. But our ancients had it.

To begin with, they said that the main purpose of a marriage is the procreation of healthy progeny – hence they followed the (1) 'Varna-Ashrama dharma' and (2) 'Gotra-system' in marriages to avoid mental (also physical) diseases for future generations.

(If you don't know, Varna = Profession, Ashrama = Phase in life, related to age, and Dharma = duty, privilege, responsibility, and right together. Following 'Varna-Ashrama dharma' is strictly living according to these factors. Gotra-system = lineage: Two people from the same Gotra marrying can cause genetic disorders in their offspring).

Ancients said the female had a sacred and secret ability (an internal arbitrary decision) to choose the best sperm among the billions coming from the Fallopian tube. The egg cell of a Dharmic wife has that intelligence. The result? A mentally healthy child.

I can hear you say: "Udayji, you are telling ridiculous, illogical, irrational non-sense. Unbelievable…"

Wait a minute.

The latest research by scientists in the University of East Anglia in collaboration between Natural Environment Research Council (NERC) the Norwegian Institute for Nature Research and the Institute of Zoology revealed how females select the 'right' sperm to fertilize their eggs when faced with the risk of being fertilized by wrong sperm from a different species.

The ancients even suggest the best time for conception. Ancient scriptures like Boudhãyana Grihya Sutra says that "one should approach his wife from the fourth to the sixteenth night, especially the later ones". Apastamba Grihya Sutra clearly says that the baby conceived on 12-16 days after the period must be healthy.

The first three months after fertilization is most important in developing or formation of the mind, so the elder women in the family would take care of the bride with a set of dos and don'ts – what to eat, whom to talk to, what to listen, etc.

Science says babies can recognize their mother's voice, which shows that they developed that memory before they were born, so the brain was 'working' at that stage. This is one of the reasons why diet and the lifestyle choices that you make can have such an impact upon the unborn child.

Our ancestors said that listening to proper Vedic mantras has a neuro-linguistic effect on the child and its brain development. There are some other rituals (Samskārs) for Hindus like Pumsavana and Sîmantonnayana during this period (partly superstitious and partly scientific but some of the rituals impact the mind of the pregnant mother and child).

Pumsavana Simantonayana is similar to the baby shower ritual observed in other parts of the world. Pumsavana literally means "quickening a being ", and it is usually translated as "quickening a male or female fetus, bringing forth a male or female baby". Pumsavana is a rite of passage observed when the pregnancy begins to show, typically in or after the third month of pregnancy and usually before the fetus starts moving in the womb. The Sîmantonnayana (ceremony of parting the hair) should take place in the sixth or eighth month (of pregnancy). But nowadays both are combined in most of the places.

If you take care of the pregnant mother properly, the child will have a healthy mind.

Incidentally, just for your reference, according to Krishna (in Bhagavad Gita), anger is the biggest mental disease and enemy of humanity.

Now, let's look at the second one: Arjita (earned, acquired, or obtained).

What are the "Arjita" reasons for the mental disorders? They are broadly divided into five – Ahara (food), vidyabhyasa (study), maithuna (mating), nidra (sleep) and vyavasaya (job, business – occupational).

(1) Ahara (Food): According to ancients, the major (from 70-90 percent) reasons for mental disorders are derived from food. Ayurveda also says the same.

The Upanishads say that the mind depends upon the food for its formation. The chemicals in the food affect mental development. "Mind is manufactured out of the food that we take" or "Mind is made up of food" quotes Chandogya Upanishad (6.5.4) saying as the conclusion of the sages' research.

Quality of mind depends upon the quality of food. Sattvic (fresh produce, freshly prepared) diet calms the mind. Rajasic (over tasty and stimulating food) diet excites the mind. Tamasic (stale or preserved food, pieces of a dead body) diet destroys the mind. Different foods produce different effects in different compartments of the brain, they say.

"When the food is pure, the whole nature becomes pure; when the nature becomes pure, the memory becomes firm" (Chhandogya Upanishad, 7.26.2)

In a practical sense, what they say about the food is true. For instance, some foods make you constipated. Just observe your performance in the office or outside when you are constipated. To know more about food, search for "Viruddha Ahara" (incompatible foods) on Google. Take care of your food, you will be saved from most of the mental disorders.

(2) Education: As the base scale of life is money today, the sole purpose of education has become 'making money. You can't blame anyone for this. In ancient days, the purpose of education was to develop wisdom and commonsense – which are totally lacking now. You are studying something incompatible with your geographical area, language, climate, time zone, etc., that would create conflict in ancestral genetic nature.

As also, we are conditioned from childhood with non-sensical beliefs and illogical concepts based upon the religion or cult in which we are born. This won't allow us to see things objectively or as is. So, what we study outside the classroom is also in conflict with the reality of the universe. A conditioned mind – especially with religious moral concepts – will definitely result in a stressful life. If you don't get scientific and rational education, you are likely to become prone to mental disorders.

(3) Maithuna (mating) is a physical necessity for a human being, the ancients said. If this need is not met properly it can create a lot of mental disorders. That's why our ancestors insisted on marriage.

Vedic scriptures made it mandatory that only married people – husband and wife – have the right to any sacraments and profession. Unmarried priests were not allowed in temples to perform main offerings to the deity. Almost all great sages were married. There was no coronation allowed for unmarried King. Why? Sex is an important part of our life. Suppressing it will only create the likes of those pervert bachelor priests and Godmen who are involved in sexual scandals.

Ancients calculated a female's healthy life expectancy roughly as first menstruation into six. If a female gets the first period at the age of 16, she would live healthy (depending on other factors too) up to 96, they said.

Today, what happens? Thanks to artificial harmonized foods, girls are getting the first period as early as at the age of 7 and develop many systemic diseases when they reach their early 40s (Similarly, among boys, sperm production starts at a very early stage). They may not die, thanks to modern medicines.

A girl gets her first period at the age of 8 means, which means according to the biological clock, she is ready to conceive. But according to our social calendar system, she is not. And most of them marry around 25. Hence from the age of 8 to 25, biologically she is with the emotions, thoughts, and enzymes, etc which are produced to make her ready for conceiving – which also means there could be an urge for maithuna (sexual activity). Just imagine how many conflicts it will create directly and indirectly in the mind? If she is not taught about these aspects scientifically, she might go into immature relationships and her life may be ruined. The same situation goes for boys too.

(4) Nidra (Sleep). You know it. A sound sleep will give you a sound mind. According to our ancestors, late sleepers and those who sleep even after sunrise would develop tamasic qualities are guaranteed candidate for mental disorders for himself/herself or the next generation for sure. Ancient health sciences advise us to go to bed early and get up early.

(5) The fourth one – occupational stress. I don't think anyone needs an explanation here. Everybody knows about such. Here also money is the sole aim, hence we are not dedicated and devoted to our karma. Everybody knows it creates disorders.

How to manage these mental aberrations?

Take up a diary, note down each thing happening concerning your mind in daily life – be honest to yourself. What food you ate in the morning and how your mind was. What were your concepts and beliefs so far, and how did they conflict with reality? How did you suppress/express your sexual feelings and what's the reaction of the mind? When did you sleep yesterday, what time you got up? The status of your mind that day. What happened in the office or business place? How did it affect you?

Why should you self-check? There is only one person that can understand you perfectly – that is you. Only you can handle your stress and frustration. And if it is serious, go to a psychiatrist or psychologist. Don't go to those magicians in the name of Godmen/God women or priests.

"Okay, I understand these things Uday, but whatever happened has happened. We cannot rectify the reasons, whether it is natural or acquired. In that case, what will I do now?" a friend asked me after we discussed these aspects.

"Simple. Tune your life rhythm according to Sun's energy. Get up early morning – before 5 AM. Light a lamp in front of your favorite god or Holy book or even your pic (if you don't believe in god). Go for a walk sometime and be one with the nature around us. Enjoy sunlight. If possible do some yoga or exercise and take rhythmic deep breathes. (Careful, before doing any breathing exercises, consult your doctor, it can damage your lungs and heart). When a thought of "I", "me" and "mine" comes, replace it with "we" and "us". Listen to some Vedic chants or songs like Vishnu Sahasranamam. Eat only Sattvik food, Avoid eating or major activities after sunset. If you observe these pointers, almost 70 percent of your mental disorders will be self-rectified on their own in 41 days," I said.

"If it still persists?"

"Go and consult a decent, professional psychologist instead of Godmen or priests."

CHAPTER - 10

Stress-busting: Cross-over Your Mind

Two months ago, a friend in Mumbai called me: "My cousin, Vijay (not real name) is suffering from some mental problems – facing extreme anxiety and depression and can't lead a quality life anymore. He is an IIT product and was running an ITES business successfully, and now is totally broken...."

"He should consult a good psychiatrist..." I said.

"He did. But the problem is that every month the drug dosage gradually goes up. I am scared that he will end up as a vegetable or a zombie on account of increasing the dosage of psychiatric drugs. You are doing research on ancient scriptures about the mind and you have cured the case of Ms.X (can't reveal the name), that's why I am approaching you..." he said.

"It was accidental. Sometimes people get cured due to their good karma and divine grace – I just share the wisdom of our ancestors, so some people may get benefited. It is just a happening by chance." I said.

"There is nothing wrong in taking any such chances now. Please..." he was insisting, almost pleading. Usually, I don't take up any such cases until and unless I intuitively feel to do so.

However, I agreed. Vijay came to see me. He is an intelligent person. Thanks to Google, he knows everything about psychology and medicines. That means his mind is full. Trying anything is like pouring water into a full cup. Before I counsel him, he has to empty his cup.

So, I changed the subject and I told him about my discussion with my late friend Mohammed Khalid about a dream he had.

"Recently I saw a tiger is chasing to eat me and I am trying to escape by running…" he had said.

"Ok, in your dream, you are being chased by a tiger. So, there is a person, who is running, experiencing…and the experience is appearing as real, otherwise, how could you feel fear, palpitations, and sweat? The experiences in the dreams are mostly real…For instance, if you are kicking in the dream you may raise your legs… it is so real…so you were running; it was for real at that point of time."

"Yes – I understand your point…"

"Who is seeing that? One person should see that…Just like you are seeing a video shoot of yours."

"Yes."

"One person is experiencing. Then, the second person is seeing it. The seer, right? The seer is just a reporter of the event; he is not affected by that. So, someone in you, let's call You No:1 is experiencing the incident with all its intensity. You No: 2 is seeing it, without any strings attached to it. You No: 2 is indifferent, yet compassionate. Right?"

"Yes."

"But the matter of fact is that you were just lying in this bed and dreaming. You were neither there running, nor seeing it. You were here and now, just in bed dreaming, this morning. You No: 3, right?"

"Yes, that is very simple to understand Udayji."

"So, tell me who is the real you? You No: 1, 2, or 3?"

"I think all three together…'

"No, in fact, there is you no.4 too. It is the wakeful state. You No: 1 = experiencer. 'You No': .2 = the seer. You No: .3. = The dreamer who was lying in the bed and sleeping. And 'You No': 4. You are woken up and now talking to me…"

"Wow."

"Now tell me, who are you?" I asked

"I am 'You No': 4"

"Is there a possibility of a 'You No': 5? – a detached self in the fifth dimension who can see the entire life of you – from birth to death – just like a dream…"

"I didn't think in that line. It should be some mind game…" Vijay stated.

"Vijay, nobody can define or learn about the whole mind – there are multiple dimensions and layers that may not be seen or felt. All these dimensions are interlinked and complicated. The more you learn, the more is the confusion. Though we know nothing, we believe all our thoughts are true and take the mind for granted. We forget mind is just another organ and is conditioned by the inputs it has received. It doesn't have any power of its own. It is just a thought-producing factory. If you chase your thoughts, your mind will become more powerful. By trusting thoughts, you are giving more energy to your mind…"

"Yes – my mind is really troubling me…"

"As long as you have a mind, it will trouble you. The "mind-control" is just a gimmick – a hot-selling commodity in the fake spirituality or personality-development business. The way out – either you have to empty your mind or should reach the status of "no-mind" or cross-over the mind"

He thought for a while and asked: "But, how to go about it?"

"Our ancestors said that the mind and body are the same. The mind is the subtle part of the body and the body is the crude part of the mind. They had divided the mind into four: Manas (sensory, processing mind), Chitta (storage of images), Ahamkara ("I-maker" or Ego), and Buddhi (that which knows, decides, judges, and discriminates). There are thousands of millions of programs that are running in between these sectors."

"I didn't know all those things…"

" Our ancestors said in Chandogya Upanishad that Mind is made of food – hence, from the purity of food follows the purity of mind. However, now that you have already spoiled the organ (mind), you might need to reverse the process…"

"But the damage has already happened…I know about neuro-psychiatric disorders and dynamic and genetic brain maps, so I know what damage the drug abuse can cause. It already has been mapped."

"But by divine grace, you can definitely make alterations. Please try to live a life in sync with your actual DNA characteristics. Try to invoke the powers that are lying dormant in your genes. For which, you need to focus on Sattvik lifestyle…"

Our ancestors have developed a perfect lifestyle to insulate from mind-body sickness – it includes (not limited to) the Sattvik lifestyle, food, yoga, pranayama, and dhyana. I talked to him about the real self and the conditioned manifested self of the same person. I explained to him the difference between the real self and manifested self. I told him how to overcome the subtle ego and conditioning of the mind. And, we sat together and prepared a schedule and timetable.

He called me yesterday – he said this is for the first time in the last two years that the doctor didn't increase the dosage! That's good news indeed. I know he can taper his medicines in due course of time. I am sure that in one year's time he will considerably reduce dependency on drugs. When you are dedicated, devoted, and determined on doing a sadhana (penance) with a sattvic lifestyle, an un-explainable grace will guide you!

CHAPTER - 11

*Stress and Anxiety, and Depression
- Easy Way to Manage Your Mind*

After writing the article "A depressed girl and the butterfly effect", I have not touched this subject for a long time. But an interesting case came up a couple of months ago.

Ashwin (not real name), a software engineer working in Sunnyvale and my regular reader, visited me two months ago.

A curious case. He said: "They have started treating me for dysthymia. I met a lot of doctors; I was diagnosed with bipolar disorder, anxiety neurosis, and major depression respectively. I tried many things - Yoga, meditation, pranayama, prayers, alternative medicines, holistic, Ayurveda, Homeopathy...Now I am on modern psychiatric drugs and heavy anti-depressants... The dosage is getting heavier...I think I have no scope in life...I am scared but getting suicidal thoughts...I have come to meet you as a last resort."

I have put in the disclaimer. "I am not a counselor. Nor a psychiatrist or psychologist. Not a healer or miracle maker. I don't even believe in spiritual healing. I am just an ordinary human being."

"But Uday Sir, you have researched our ancient scriptures. You are blessed with our ancestral wisdom. I came to you with a hope that you will have some solution..."Ashwin said.

"Ashwin, I have not researched psychology. My subject is only the mind. However, I know that most forms of mental illness can be cured. Depression also has a cure. It is difficult (but not impossible) to come out of such disorders. Preliminary research has shown that chronic depression can cause reduction the volume of grey matter in the brain and cause brain inflammation which may make it difficult to treat depression. Further, long term use of certain anti-depressants may cause some intense withdrawal effects for longer periods when people taking them try to taper it off. This may make people to continue treatment to reduce these withdrawal effects and hence be dependent on medicines. Yet, these findings cannot form the basis to go off treatment for moderate and severe depression which if untreated can lead to debilitating effects and suicide in many cases. However, adhering to a life-style prescribed our ancients, may work towards preventing depression or recovering from it before it worsens."

"I have no scope in my life. I am done for. I am scared to commit suicide and I am scared of even thinking about it. But eventually, I will have to do it...I need some help here, Uday sir," his eyes were tearful.

I remembered my mother's words: "If somebody comes for specific and genuine help do not ignore them. Do whatever you can."

Suddenly I said: "Our ancestors knew the reasons for the mental illness. They have provided a solution that would prevent such diseases. This much I know. But curing a disease is a doctor's job."

"Okay, sir. At least tell me, what's the reason for the diseases?"

"Our ancestors classified the mental diseases into two category - (1) Naisargika (natural) and (2) Aarjitham (Accrued or earned)"

"Okay"

I have explained about it. (See above).

"There are three subdivisions in Naisargika (natural) mental illness. Mathrujam (the genes from the mother), Pithrujam (the genes from the father), and Atmajam (Came via Atma. Atma doesn't have an English word. So let's call it inner-self). After thousands of years, modern psychiatry has proven the first two as scientific truth. But science doesn't approve of the "Atma" factor. In due course, they might. So, for the time being, Atmajam is a belief, though I know it exists."

"Okay. What's Aarjitham?"

"The accrued illness comes from 'Annaiam' (acquired from the food we take in) and 'Salmyajam' (acquired from the atmosphere). The first one - that is mental illness can accrue from the food - is not proven by science. The second one - every being is influenced by the atmosphere it is brought up in, like the home, school, village, country, religion, community, etc., and the habits of the grownups there. The modern science calls it as social conditioning."

"Uday sir, what's the solution?"

"Let's discuss Naisargika first. It is important to have born to good parents with good genes. So, in those days, people were looking for things like lineage, hierarchy (Gotra), pedigree, family background, etc. for marriage so that the couple will have healthy and good progeny. Now those things are replaced by money, power, and external looks. Today, you are free to choose your spouse; it's a basic individual's freedom. But, then your selection could be based on little or no experience and a narrow understanding of life. What's more is that you are conditioned with the wrong concept of love and marriage by the media (movies, stories, and advertisements). So, you could end up marrying the wrong person without checking his/her ancestry. The result? Innocent children may suffer."

"In fact, my parents had so-called love marriage..."Ashwin said.

"Now you cannot do anything about it. We do not know if one of your parents carried that dangerous DNA with him/her..."

"And Atma?"

"They say, good Atma is the result of good karma. Good karma is dependent on one's dharma. Dharma is founded upon Varna. A person earnestly following his/her Varna would be a dedicated, devoted, and determined doer. He/she will produce only good karmic power. There will not be any conflicts with innate nature as the person's Karma is based on his/her karma. Our ancestors believed that at least you can do good karma in this life, so that, an unknown living being that will have your Atma in future will be good..."

"Oh, so if my illness was natural, there is no remedy?"

"As I said, our ancestors focus more on the prevention aspects rather than cure. They have provided you with dharmic principles, which, of course, were not followed. There are cures in Ayurveda. But I am very skeptical about it. Hardly anybody practices pure, real Ayurveda nowadays. Most of the herbs and medicines are not available. The real Ayurveda combined with some holistic lifestyle that includes pranayama, yoga, dhyana, and to an extent prayer (the power of prayers, again, not proven scientifically. But it may have at least some placebo effect in the mind) can do some help...."

"What if it is accrued?"

"Yes, it might have been accrued from food habits. No psychiatrist will ask you about the food you eat before diagnosing your illness. But we are what we eat, says our ancestors. Food consumption should be based on profession (Varna), life, time, place, family, age, gender, and individual. "From earth herbs, from herbs food, from food seed, from seed man. Man thus consists of the essence of food" (Taittiriya Upanishad). "

"Yes, I have read your article about our ancestors who have done extensive research for thousands of years and found that what we eat determines our mental as well as physical state."

"Yes, they have developed a unique and important concept of Viruddhahara (dietetic incompatibility). There are 18 categories of Viruddhahara. They say insanity derives from food...."

"As you said earlier, it is not scientifically proven..."

"Science has proven it. When you eat food NOT according to your karma, problems can pop up. For instance, a stockbroker sitting in front of a computer (Vysya) and a person who does physical labor in the agricultural land (farmer) have different dietary requirements. Our ancestors told it in a different language. So, it is very important to check if you eat the compatible food."

"You said about the atmosphere..."

"Yes. Atmosphere influences a lot. For instance, parenting. Both parents are working and the child is thrown at the mercy of a maid or playschool. The child will surely develop a lot of psychological issues. Pampering has created arrogant and adamant kids. In school and colleges, nobody teaches you common sense. Your job is to mugging-up theories and thoughts of somebody which has nothing to do with bare life here. Modern education takes you away from the soil and sun. It's like cutting off the roots, which will create conflicts in you... Nobody teaches you the values of giving and co-existing. All they teach you superficial etiquettes. They inflate your ego in the name of personality development. You learn only to compete. All these things will create mental illness..."

"But we have spiritual and religious life..." Ashwin asked in between.

"I am not spiritual, so I can't talk about the spiritual life. Religions are multi-level marketing set up that thrive on superstitions. So, religion is NOT going to help you anyways..."

"What about belief in God?"

"90% of the people who have mental illness are strong believers. Why is it that belief in God didn't save them? The religious fundamentalists, fanatics, and terrorists are huge believers. They are lunatics too. So how can you say belief in God can save you from any mental illness?"

"So god can't help?"

"Yes, if you can experience God or divinity, it is the best solution. You will have to realize that God is inside as well as outside. You should realize that you are a part of the divine cosmos. You must know that you are pure and divine. That's IMPOSSIBLE as long as you have concepts or ego. Your mind is fully conditioned with a lot of concepts or assumptions about God, depending upon the religion or region you had been brought up."

"Yes"

"Concepts and memories form a strong belief system and ego. The ego will always create noise and conflicts. A person with an ego cannot realize God. The moment you reach an egoless state, you can feel the presence of God."

"How to reach an egoless state?"

"It is very simple and easy. Just be aware. Create awareness in you. When you are aware of the divine you and experience the divine existence around you, your thoughts-producing factory will stop. No thoughts = mind is calm and relaxed. You will feel the stillness inside. Peace and happiness. Our ancestors developed thousands of methods for it. Have you read Gitas? (Ancient pearls of wisdom)?"

"Bhagavad Gita?"

"Not just that. There are nearly 40 Gitas that reveal ancient wisdom. You may search and find a method of your choice...Each has different sadhana (practice). Because every individual is unique. A person is perfect with his/her imperfections..."

I talked to him for more than two hours. Mostly, about his family and ancestry only. We could locate the root cause of the diseases - it was accrued. We have formulated a sadhana that is useful for him. He is continuing his Sadhana. I am sure he can manage his problems.

CHAPTER - 12

The Angry Young Woman

"Sir, I am a working woman. I am facing a miserable life condition due to my anger and irritation. I have to cook food for my two school-going children, my husband, and his parents. No one is here to help me with the morning chores. Even the servant woman comes late when I finish all my work. When I am busy in the kitchen my in-laws also get up and ask for coffee. Kids won't listen to me and are not properly organized. My husband also pressurizes me while I work. I leave the house at around 8.30 AM on the company bus. Some male co-workers make advances towards me while traveling and in the office, it's also totally irritating. My boss is also a mean person who unnecessarily pressurizes me. Many times, I feel like a pressure cooker about to burst from inside. I am not able to cope up with this. When I read a few articles on your website, I felt like you can help me. Please spend a few minutes addressing this issue, Sir. How to manage my anger and irritation?" a pretty long question from a reader.

It is normal for people to get angry. But if it persists for more than 30 seconds, it will turn into a disease.

Our ancestors, especially Krishna, said: "From anger arises delusion, from delusion, comes memory-loss, from loss of memory, the intellect is destroyed. When the intellect is destroyed, there is a loss of reason (lack of discrimination) which ruins a person!" (Bhagavad Gita).

Science says anger is a chemical reaction of hormones and neurotransmitters. It triggers increased platelet activation and thrombosis, increases vulnerability to illnesses, compromises the immune system. The results are very dangerous.

So, somehow we have to manage anger. If your anger sustains, it becomes the biggest and severe mental disease. Then you need help from psychologists, or counselors, or doctors.

How do we get angry? When someone or something acts or says NOT according to our expectation. Or when our desire is not met. All waves of anger come under this category. However, there are other deep-rooted psychological reasons like suppression of sadness in childhood and hurt of ego or created reasons like pushing everything to the last moment. That we have to look into separately. This answer is for the questioner.

"Somehow, you have to manage anger. I know it is not easy when you live life like a pressure cooker..." I said.

"Are there any sadhanas, kriyas to prevent or manage anger?"

"Yes, but it works like a vaccine to prevent disease. Here, you already have the disease."

"What to do then?" she asked.

1. When you get angry, physically move away from the place you're standing or sitting. Take ten steps.

2. Change the work you have been doing – from cutting vegetables to washing clothes, maybe.

3. Consciously change the thought pattern – think of a pleasant or happy moment in the past. See a comedy program. Listen to melody – anything to deviate your thoughts.

4. Write down your thoughts, feelings, and activities during the anger. The next day, when you get time, read it to yourself. This is the only way to reach the subconscious mind and convince it that anger is not good.

5. When you get angry at your child, for instance, when he has

broken a glass worth Rs 20, compare values. Is your child's worth less than Rs 20? Respond or advise him after some time, when you cool down.

6. Everyone has a limitation. Do the work within your limits only and don't overstretch. Tell your husband or in-laws clearly that this is as much as you can work. I need help from you. Everyone needs to work in a family and share it accordingly. No work is confined to wife or husband.

7. Our ancestors warned us against "Prati kriya" (react) and advised us to follow "Anu Kriya" (respond). Prati means against or in opposition with. An action against something is a reaction. Anu means after, along with, or further. Kriya means just action. So, both words include action which is needed in every situation. It's not the situation, but whether we react (negative) or respond (positive) to the important situation. As you know life is 10% of what happens to you and 90% of how you react to it. It's about what you do with what happens. Many times, a strong, discouraging look at your co-worker might stop them.

8. Usually, we get angry at people whom we think lesser than us or at those whom we think we have dominance over. For instance, you can cook a good dish, but your son can't. That doesn't mean son is lesser than you. Please understand that everyone has some unique talents that are better than you.

9. Switch off your mobile or turn it into airplane mode (if you are listening to music). Never ever respond to SMS or WhatsApp messages or even voice calls when you are angry.

10. Lastly, begin a long-term plan, that would work as a vaccine later – it includes, exercise, sattvic food, dhyana, pranayama, yoga, etc. It would bring you back to a healthy condition – physically and mentally.

CHAPTER - 13

Don't Do Something Permanently Stupid Just Because You Are Temporarily Upset

Gracy Wilson, my media friend in the UK, is a very hot-tempered person.

She has issues with the editor, management, and most of the people she meets. She reacts to each and everything in life. She just can't tolerate any injustice and unethical activities.

We were connected through social media. She went through my website.

We had a long chat about life and its beauty. She asked me: "You are telling me not to react, but to respond. Every situation in life is different. How to respond? Where to react? And how will we know whether it is a reaction or response? It is easy for you to write or preach. But you can't walk the talk..."

"Hmm..." I keyed in.

"I am a responsible person," she said.

"Responsibility = ability to respond," I said.

She didn't say anything for a moment. Then she said: "I know my short-coming. I know I react instantly and do not respond properly. I really don't understand the difference..."

"Oh, what's there to understand? The reaction is automatic and usually immediate - it comes from the emotions; it lacks control. A response includes action, but can be and usually is considered, and not necessarily immediate. When you respond, that means you are in control. When you react, that means that you have surrendered control to someone else...And most of the time, a sudden reaction creates permanent damage in human relationships or life. Sometimes it ruins our/others' entire life..." I said.

"Ok..."

"When a doctor tells you are reacting to the medicine that's a bad sign, isn't it? When he tells you are responding to the medicine, you take it as a good sign..."

"You're right Uday, you have a point there..."

"Reaction comes out of your past conditionings; it is mechanical. The response comes out of your presence, awareness, consciousness; it is non-mechanical."

"I am Master's in English, so I know the definitions and explanations of both. My question was how to respond, and not react?" she got impatient and began reacting.

"Our natural instinct is to react. A natural inclination towards responding, however, comes with time and practice. You have to develop awareness..."

"Now you are talking...please continue..."

"My ancestors have called it "Prati kriya" (react) and "Anu Kriya" (respond) in Sanskrit. Prati means against or in opposition with. An action against something is a reaction. Anu means after, along, or further. Kriya means just action. So, both words include action which is needed in every situation. It's not the situation, but whether we react (negative) or respond (positive) to the important situation. As you know the life is 10% of what happens to you and 90% of how you react to it. It's about what you do with what happens." I said.

"Ok, ok, don't talk too much of philosophy... but how to practice it?"

"When anything happens ask yourself four questions - Was it intentional? Is this really a big deal? Am I in automatic mode or aware? Is this worth ruining a relationship over? Then mostly you would find forgiveness is a good choice."

"But when it is needed to be countered by an action?"

"As a first step, give space and create a gap between you and the stimulus. Then put yourself in the other persons' shoes - How would you like to be treated if it were you...Ask yourself - am I reacting? Simply asking yourself that question can ground you and give you a quick mental break to perhaps choose differently"

"In case, I am getting an urgent phone call on mobile?"

"If you do not know how to respond, try not to pick up the call until and unless it is a life-and-death issue. Similarly, do not reply to SMS immediately. Keep a gap between any communications"

"That's a great idea. Coming back to life situation, what should I do instead of my hot-tempered scolding?"

"It's not just what you say but how you say it. Be careful about the tone you use while speaking to someone over an incident that may have upset you. Be polite, but firm."

"Hmmm...But it is difficult as the situation is different in different contexts..." she said.

"Any given situation is a fact. It is just an objective fact when you perceive it without a reaction. A reaction is the incapacity to accept the fact. When you react, you do not see the fact. If you accept the fact AS IS and without your interpretation, you can see that you can act in both ways - one is the reaction, another is the response...This awareness will come to you."

"Be specific, if my editor scolds me, how can I respond?" she asked.

"Ok - your editor calls you idiot. If you are not an idiot, why should you react? That's his perception or opinion. Why should you try to change it? And if you are really an idiot, he is making a true statement of fact. Why should you react or respond?"

"Uday, that's a pathetic joke. If he calls me names?"

"If he calls you a monkey, look at the mirror and make sure that you don't look like a monkey. Then politely tell him to have his eyes checked and you don't see any monkeys around..."

She sent a laughing smiley.

"Gracy, we all make mistakes, we all say dumb things occasionally, and we're only human after all. So, in the event of you reacting emotionally, apologize to people. Not only is it important to apologize to the other person, but it is also important to forgive yourself. Always respond intelligently even when you face to unintelligent treatment. Please don't do something permanently stupid just because you are temporarily upset" I said.

Me, is the inner me - that is what I am. There is also an outward Me, that I project (manifest) for others. Between these, there is a difference. In my job, I sometimes have to act furious, when I am actually cool and collected.

CHAPTER - 14

*Problems Are Mandatory,
Worrying Is Optional*

A man was standing near a beautiful beach. He wanted to take bath in the ocean - a calm ocean without waves, to be precise. So, he waited for the waves to stop to take bath.

Will he be successful?

All of us know the answer: "No."

All of you would say: "He is not going to take bath at all. Doesn't he know waves won't stop? He is a fool."

It is very easy to see the other's foolishness. But when it comes to us, we won't see our foolishness.

This is what I told my friend when we talked about his marriage. He wants to get married. He is already 36. He has many problems, he says - family, social, professional, health, neighbors, relatives...quite a lot of problems. Sometimes he feels like committing suicide - because there seems no end or solutions to his problems in life.

He is leading a miserable life. So, he is suppressing his need for marriage.

"How can I marry Sir? Without peace of mind, how can I? It's my destiny, sir. Please can you help me solve my problems? I want to settle down everything and lead a peaceful married life..."

I couldn't help laughing - he talks as if marriage would bring in peace! But he came to me seeking solace. Peace of mind is irrespective of whether you're married or not.

That's when I told him about the man on the beach. I told him about an incident with a management guru. He was staying in the same hotel and someone introduced me to him.

This guru appeared to be pious, calm, peaceful, and composed. One day I met him in a business class hotel. He was there for his one-day program on "How to avoid stress and cope up with situations"

He was totally upset and tensed. I asked him why. He said: "What to say yaar? Only a few seats are sold for tomorrow's program. I don't know what to do?"

"Relax Guru. You can find a solution for this..." I said.

"What solution yaar? I already paid for the hall and publicity...If people don't turn up, I would be in a great soup..." he was behaving like he is going to have a panic attack!

Problems, problems everywhere. Not a single solution for the problems!

"Yes, yes, that's my problem...there is no solution at all..." my friend (who is about to get married to find peace in life) said.

"You are wrong. Every problem comes with a clear solution. If you are becoming part of the problem and giving energy to it, how can you become part of the solution?"

"I am giving energy to problems?"

"When you keep on worrying about your problems, you are giving energy to it. Let the problem exists. It is like waves in the ocean..."

Before me completing it, he said: "You don't know Uday sir. You have not faced such problems..."

I laughed out loud: "You think I have not faced any problems in my life? You are wrong. I have faced much more problems than you can ever imagine. I had lived a life of stress and tension...I still have problems..."

"You are a blessed man...God will listen to your prayers..."

"I don't pray to God to solve my problems. It is not god's duty to find solutions to the problems that we create" I said.

"Then?"

"I would rather tell the problem: See Mr.Problem, I have God with me, so don't threaten me."

A smile came to his tensed face.

"But seriously sir, how did you solve it?"

"Let's welcome the problems. It is like waves. It won't stop. It is foolish to think that a day will come without having problems. When one problem is solved, another will pop up. 'Lived happily-ever-after' is just a phrase that appears in bedtime stories. You are a bigger fool to wait for problems to cease. It won't."

Almost 99 percent of the problems have a solution. We, with our limited (conditioned mind), sometimes won't be able to find a solution. So, we need to talk to our elders - our parents, elderly relatives, teachers, friends, or to any of your well-wishers. Don't be so egoistic to think that I can find a solution on my own. Sometimes, the solution will be ridiculously simple, but we can't or won't see it, I told him.

When I talked to him, I understood that all his problems are a manifestation of his ego, conditioned mind, perception, and attitude. He wants to make changes in others, whereas the simple solution was that he should change. Mostly, we cannot change a given situation, but we can change our attitude towards it.

"I can guarantee you. You will have problems till you die. It is not worth wasting our life to think about problems. It's better to acknowledge the problems that we have and start living with the problem. You can declare peace with the problem and live happily. If you think that peace would come only after solving the problem, you are like that man on the beach who is waiting for waves to stop," I said.

Start loving problems. Live with problems. And live as a troubleshooter!

Problems in life are mandatory. But worrying about them is optional.

CHAPTER - 15

Are You a Free Thinker?

What is the highest state a human can reach? Or what is the ultimate aim of a human being?

Happiness? Peace? Heaven? God? Comforts? Bliss? Ecstasy

Oh, No.

According to our ancients, the ultimate aim is to be a free thinker. You can't believe it? Before going to that, a simple question.

Are you a free thinker?

99% would answer YES. "Oh, I have my own way of thinking. I think independently. No one can influence my thoughts," you would say.

But the truth is NO. Our mind is so manipulated that we don't even know that we are conditioned to be a slave thinker.

If you have ever listened to the Vedic mantras during any ritual/ceremony, you might have come across the Sanskrit phrase "Vairagya Sidhyartham" (to achieve Vairagya). All your offerings are done NOT to please God, or go to heaven, or fulfilling any wishes, but for developing a state of being called Vairagya.

What's Vairagya?

There is a popular misconception – Vairagya means "detachment."

"According to our sages, get yourself detached from the bondage and material life, then you will get happiness or moksha," many would say.

If someone tells you to get detached from material life, you can ROFL (rolling on the floor, laughing). It is a huge joke.

Our body is full of chemical actions. Even thinking about "detachment" is chemical action. Living is a chemical process. Pure chemistry. Material science.

Detaching from material life is, well, they are asking you to commit suicide. Probably they are blind to the superstition of heaven – life after death in heaven. There is nothing like that.

Ask yourself. Why are our Gods and Goddesses are wearing a lot of ornaments? Why do they carry metal weapons? Aren't those materials? I have already explained the science behind many concepts of God.

But those Gurus would advise you that you are happy only when you cut off your material life and bondage. They call it "detachment". It's again a conditional life then. If you are getting happiness from the 'detachment', it ONLY means you are really attached to the detachment.

But it is NOT free thinking. You should be happy in attachment as well as in detachment, that is when you really become "free". In other words, if you are free from the bondage of attachment as well as detachment, then you are qualified to be a Vairagi or 'free thinker'.

It is NOT easy to be a free thinker.

I have been born and bought up in the cradle of Marxism/ Communism. Most of my friends were Communist Marxists. But it is quite impossible to argue, debate, or discuss with my Marxist friends. When they don't have a reply, they will get angry, will take it personally, and start hating you – or even physically attack you. Why? They are so much attached to their ideology and think it is correct. The more dedicated they are, they would get angrier

(I am not talking about today's Marxists who are hypocrites seeking pleasure and comforts in an American way). It goes the same for people who believe in other ideologies too. Can they ever be free thinkers? NO.

Religion is another slave-maker. The moment you talk about anything related to the illogical beliefs or superstitions in religions, they would become very angry. Any fanatic believer of any religion gets angry when their superstitious beliefs are questioned. Why? They blindly think their dearest beliefs are true.

But all of them, whether conditioned by ideology or religion, are rational enough to find faults with other ideologies or religions. So, even a rational thinker cannot be a free thinker.

Yes, a rational thinker can be a logical thinker, but he/she is NOT a free thinker. Why? A rationalist's brain (mind) is so conditioned that he/she thinks every learning is true.

The moment you break from the conditioning and think without any prejudice or color, you become a free thinker. The moment you become a free thinker, you will be the happiest man.

For instance, Krishna was a free thinker. He didn't have any inhibitions. Even after revealing the greatest philosophy of life, the Gita, he said, "Arjuna, I told you what I felt right. It is up to you to follow it or not."

He neither threatened by commanding you, "This is a Holy book. if you don't follow my words, I will roast you in the hellfire," nor promised to reserve a seat in heaven if you follow him.

What's more, he went on to say that we shouldn't try to change another person's mindset. And that's the extent of free-thinking!

CHAPTER - 16

How to Overcome Depression without Medication?

In my WhatsApp Broadcast, queries on depression top all the subject lines among the readers' messages. Long ago, I received a message from Janani (Bangalore): "Udayji, I am suffering from severe depression. I am also feeling sad or miserable most of the time. Sometimes the scary thought of suicide comes to my mind. Can you please advise me on how to cope up with depression without any medication?"

I replied: "Janani, please consult a psychologist or therapist soon. Severe depression is a leading cause of disability worldwide and is a major contributor to the overall global burden of disease. I suggest you meet a good doc ASAP..."

"Udayji, two friends of mine (she mentioned their names) said that they were able to manage their issues after reading your articles. They contacted you for your phone number. And after talking to you, they felt far better and happy..."

"I have indeed written a few articles based on our ancient scriptures and my observations and study, that's all. Yes, it might have helped a few people - I also get some letters expressing gratitude and thankfulness. And as part of my 'manava seva' mission, I spent some time with those who genuinely want to talk to me. But that doesn't make me an expert on the subject. What's more, probably those readers were having very mild depression or were in the beginning phase, hence those articles and talking to me might have helped them to sail through..."

"Hmm. Udayji, have you ever felt depressed?"

"Me? No. Never. I won't feel depressed at all, despite there were hundred genuine reasons like miseries, hardships, setbacks, and injustice happened in my life"

"How did you manage it?"

"I didn't manage anything. I am used to walking in the soil and sand without footwear. I can still walk without chappals. When I go to my family house, I move around the property without chappals so that my barefoot become soiled and dirty.."

"How's it related to depression?"

"I believe that a person who has walked barefoot on earth during childhood won't get depressed. Your body memory will recall the fact that you are from the soil and will go back to the soil. That will give you the noblest feeling of 'down to earth. That would decrease the ego part of you. Mostly, you feel depressed when you are in the over-emphasis mode of "I", "me" and "mine" in you. When you feel down to earth, you will see how blessed you are to live on this earth..."

"So, Can I walk without chappals so that I can cope up with depression"

"Janani, that's an idiotic way of looking at things. I said those who were walking on the earth barefoot have a lesser chance of getting depression or at least, I believe so. It's not scientifically proven so it's not a solution for you. As far as I know, adopting a lifestyle in tune with nature can prevent many mental illnesses including depression..."

She didn't listen to that. Instead, asked another question: "Udayji, will meditation help? I have heard that when all medicines fail and when doctors can't help, the topmost advice would be to start meditation. And many studies show meditation cured severe mental diseases."

"I do not know what you mean by meditation. There are hundreds of meditative methods available in the market. Once, while interviewing him, (late) Swami Nirmalananda Giri, the ocean of Vedic wisdom and expert in Ayurveda, told me that today's meditation methods can lead to mental diseases."

"Oh really? Shocking! Meditation won't help?"

"Today's most of the meditation techniques only address the mind. In 99% of techniques, you are asking your own conditioned mind to control it! Will it help? You have already created a demon of mind (conditioned mind) and it had taken control of you. In such a case, meditation may not help. In fact, our ancestors taught us Dhyanam. It is NOT mediation. To my understanding, meditation is the wrong English word for Dhyanam."

"So meditation is not English translation to Dhanyam..."

"No, Dhyanam helps you to cross over the mind. It will make the real self in you witness your mind, body, and surrounding. It is something about going beyond the mind. You can help your mind, only if you go beyond the mind... Dhyanam will make you happy and peaceful, always. It addresses all mental illnesses from the biggest mental ailment anger to mild diseases like anxiety. Dhyanam will also help you with your source code."

"Can you advise me how to do Dhyanam?"

"Every human being is a unique expression. You are also unique. So, without studying and researching your real nature, it would be difficult to suggest. I don't know you or your nature. So, you will have to go deeper into yourself - find out who you really are, and then you will know how to do Dhyanam... But specific to your concern, at this stage, it would be really difficult."

"How many days it will take to address depression if one starts Dhyanam?"

"That also depends. From a few seconds to a few years! It's like dissecting a Jigsaw puzzle - sometimes you can dissect it in a minute.

Sometimes it may take days together..."

"Can you at least tell me how to prevent one from getting depressed?"

"Prevention is very easy. The fundamental fact about the homo sapiens is that your DNA source code is that of tribals (any of aboriginal peoples of India). It didn't change ever since.

(1) Live life in tune with Sun. Get up early morning. Go to bed early.

(2) Your Karma and lifestyle should be in tune with your Dharma.

(3) Respect genetics - be aware that it is NOT you, but the genetic code that controls you - your body and mind are controlled by those codes.

(4) Don't try to mimic (imitate) others and adopt others' lifestyles - that include other cultures and life-style that are not suitable for the real you. It would create conflicts.

(5) Be down to earth and address your direct ego and subtle ego.

(6) Cultivate three different hobbies (a) choose anything from art and music (b) gardening and farming - if you cannot, at least visit a park or garden every day and spend some time with plants and (c) get involved in social service (at least forward helpful Dharmic messages/videos to friends and relatives).

(7) Make it a point that you do regular exercises or walk or yoga for half an hour to one hour every day.

(8) If you believe in God, light a lamp in front of its image and pray for a few minutes. The lighting of the lamp is a very important symbol that sync with your brain. If you don't believe in God, just observe sunrise or sunset.

These steps would make you strong and you will have a less chance of getting stress and mental ailments..." I said.

"So, I shall follow these steps earnestly..."

"It is NOT for you at this stage. These steps might prevent anyone from many mental diseases except those originating from other reasons (See my articles on (1) Naisargika (natural) and (2) Aarjitham (Accrued or earned) causes mental diseases). Prevention is not a cure. You're already in an advanced state. So, you MUST first consult a doctor and take care of your sickness. Once you become normal, then start this lifestyle and follow those steps, you'll be protected from further attacks. Others, who have stress, anxiety, mood swing, or initial phase of depression, can practice those steps."

CHAPTER - 17

Do Early Morning Dreams Come True?

"Sir, I have seen a nightmarish dream (terrifying dream) in the morning. A lot of people say morning dreams can come true. I am really scared. Is there anything we can do as a remedy or penance to stop it from happening? " - a reader from Bangalore? Her name is Anuradha (not real).

"Anuradha, what's the population of India?"

"Indian population is about 135 crores (1.35billion). Why?"

"Have you learned mathematics at the college level?"

"Yes sir, I am a B Tech graduate..."

"Okay. Have you learned probability theory?"

"Yes, but I don't remember."

"Oh, in probability theory, the law of large numbers is a theorem that describes the result of performing the same experiment a large number of times. It would have been easier to discuss if we remember the law. Ok, are you a working girl, Anu?"

"Yes, Uday sir," she said.

"Do you go to the office in two-wheeler?"

"Oh! Sir, do you have any magical powers? How did you know I go with my husband on a motorbike? And my dream was..."

"It's just a coincidence," I interrupted. "I have been a biker since my teenage and I still prefer to drive my bike than my car. The bike is like an extra limb for me. So, naturally, I asked if you have a two-wheeler. And in Bangalore traffic, it would be easy to cruise on a bike, so it was a simple genuine question...So, just answer my question..."

"Yes, Uday sir"

"Imagine you sit in the backseat and your husband is driving via a rough bumpy road. You have a glass full of water in your hand. What are the chances you reach the destination without losing a drop of water from the glass?"

"It is impossible sir..."

"Yes, practically chances are zero. It is almost impossible. But science doesn't have any laws to prove that it is not possible. If we apply probability theory, we can say, it is not impossible but it is improbable..."

"Uday sir, I don't understand."

"Okay, I will put it this way, an average person has three to five dreams per night, and some may have up to seven. So, let's put the number as five for easy calculation. That means in a year (365 days) you see 1825 dreams. But we won't remember most of the dreams. According to experts, we remember two dreams a week on average. That is, you remember 108 dreams in a year...Clear?"

"Yes sir."

"Indian population is 135 crores (1.35billion). That means Indian people remember 14,580 crores (145 billion) dreams a year. Given such a huge or large number, few dreams may come true (randomly). If one dream happens for real among 10 crores (that is 1 in 100 million), the total number of dreams that come to true could be, 13.5. It is so negligible."

"That's right. In a large number of 14,580 crores (145 billion), 13.5 is just a negligibly small number."

"Now, we know millions of events happen in your life. Naturally, one or two can link it up with the dreams we saw. So, the dream that comes true is just a natural probability in the law of large numbers - it is just pure applied mathematics in the realm of coincidence..."

"Oops, now I understood - so it is just a coincidence or cross-connection that one dream among billions can happen among billions of events in life..."

"Right. If one dream comes through or nearly happens that way, you might remember that dream - it is called selectivity of memory. There are impossible dreams and improbable dreams. Falling from the bike is not an improbable dream..."

"OMG, how did you know that the dream was about a bike accident? Uday sir, do you have any special power?"

"Not at all. You have given enough clues, Anu. I guess it might be a bike accident, the way you jumped gun while I talked about the bike. This is the trick that those fraud astrologers and soothsayers use to gain your trust. A bike accident may happen anytime, given the condition of roads and traffic systems there. So, there always is a fear in the subconscious. You saw it as a dream...Most of the bike drivers may see such a dream."

"Yes, but sir, you didn't say for sure if it will happen or not..."

"Ha-ha! what were we discussing? If you dream that you are riding in a space vehicle on the planet of Mars and you meet with an accident, well, it won't happen. There is no impossible event that comes true in dreams, but only improbable events. Don't worry. The dream is just a dream. Take it that way, you will be relaxed."

"But I have heard from my aunt that her early morning dream, actually came true. Is it sheer coincidence too?"

"Hmmm. Anu, I have an incident of a dream coming true in my life. During my teenage, I had seen a dream that I was sleeping near to an unknown beautiful girl, surrounded by a beautiful forest..."

"Oh, has it come true?"

"Yes...err...Almost true...There was a wall between me and her, that's all. She slept with her parents in a room and I slept with my friends in the adjacent room. There was just a wall between our cots. It was in a resort near to the forest area. Since there was a power failure, we could hear the sound of animals and other creatures - almost felt like in a forest..."

Anuradha laughed aloud.

"This is how we make our dreams appear true. It is normal for a teenager to see a beautiful girl in his dream. So, when we come into an almost similar situation, our mind cooks up, adds up the images that we saw in the dream, and co-relates those things well. Since it was an unknown face, it can fit anyone. So, even when a dream comes true, 90% would be by the instigation of mind and wild imagination...Just like you fixing up a jigsaw puzzle from nothing or with just one or two pieces."

"So, a dream coming true is a popular misconception and not exactly backed by science or evidence."

"Yes, but your dreams can come true..." I said.

"What?" shockingly she asked.

"Yes. The dreams come true only If you work on them. You try harder and give your best, maybe all your dreams might become true. Good luck."

"Oh God, I was shocked for a moment...Thank you...But during the dreaming, the experience was terribly real."

"We come in contact with real objects in the waking state, but we contact only imagined things in the dream state. While there are actual pleasure and actual pain in the waking world, there is an imagined pleasure and imagined pain in the dream world. The Sankalp (imagination in this context) has its powers. That's a different topic, we will discuss sometime."

CHAPTER - 18

What Do The Most Ancient Scriptures in the World Tell Us About the Mind?

According to Hindu scriptures, the mind is just a small part of the whole system or an inner instrument called "Antahkarana". This instrument plays four different roles:

1. Manah (Manas) is our Conscious Mind or just Mind. Mind is a loose translation of Manas. It also is our faculty of thinking as we understand it with all its qualities and expressions – it is our mental attention instrument in front of the perceived world. Mana also means mind that pops up thoughts.

2. Buddhi is our Wisdom Faculty or Intelligence. Buddhi's role is analyzing and making decisions. Buddhi is our faculty to discrimination, choice-alternative decision, or generally the capability to make decisions.

3. Chittam (Memory) is the storage section of Samskaras (memories, likes, dislikes, desires, habits) in dormant form (where inputs get conditioned as files and kept). It is a repository of memories conscious and subconscious.

4. Ahankara (Egoism). It has the role of identifying with your body-mind sense complex and gives you an "I" feeling. Ahamkara is false knowledge of self i.e. when we keep considering ourselves other than Atman (true self). Ahamkara is an ambassador of the Self in this phenomenal empirical world. Ahamkara - empirical ego is the doer of the Self.

When the brain (Masthishkam) is the active place of Mann when Mann is working with the direction/provision/use of the brain it is called Buddhi (intellect). Whenever any Samskaras get triggered, they become Vrittis (Subconscious thoughts). Samskaras get triggered due to Ahamkara.

In this state of Ahamkara, Manas (Conscious mind) keeps continuously running under control of Vrittis (subconscious thoughts). Vrittis literally means "whirlpool". It is an apt name for the waves of thought in the Chitta. Thought doesn't have any power in itself. But from the infinite storehouse of force in nature, the instrument called Chitta takes hold of some, absorbs it, and sends it out as thought. Force is supplied to us through food, and out of that food, the body obtains the power of motion, etc.

Both conscious and subconscious thoughts reflect emotions. Specifically, negative emotions block us from awareness, and also in the long term, negative emotions cause diseases in the physical body.

Here, the Manas won't help you. Instead, it keeps trying to calm down emotions, by bringing solutions from the external world through sensory pleasures. So, we see that the mind is not intelligent; yet it appears to be intelligent.

The Chitta, as said is a storage place of inputs you have received in this life and before. It just stores information as files. It won't transform you. The only way to survive this emotional outburst is to increase the clarity of Buddhi. You need light to get clarity. The light is deconditioning and awareness.

When you are aware, you have utmost clarity, which means there is no further requirement to run a conscious mind on that knowledge. That means clear knowledge brings Manas at peace.

So whenever the subconscious pushes a confused knowledge to the screen of Manas, it starts running to remove that confusion.

Clear knowledge without confusion becomes the wisdom of Buddhi. Wisdom takes you towards ultimate freedom i.e., true knowledge of self. So, wisdom washes away Ahamkara (false knowledge of self).

Our ancestors have clearly defined two ways for a human being for living: One is the path of Awareness - You bring awareness to Manas by deconditioning yourself from the inputs.

The other one is the path of Unawareness - Manas in control of Vrittis (memories and habits) conditioned. Conditioned Mind – Manas analyzing and acting based on stored data (memories & Samskaras)

The logical way would be to adapt the Path of Awareness which finally leads to even transcending and dissolving of the Manas and its associates discussed earlier, namely, Chitta and ahankara.

What's Nirvana?

This transcendence could culminate in Nirvana- a place of perfect peace and happiness. In Hindu Dharma and Buddhism, Nirvana is the highest state that someone can attain, a state of enlightenment, meaning a person's individual desires and suffering go away.

However, one cannot describe Nirvana with thought or language. That's why no one can really explain what exactly it is. They can describe things about it but Nirvana itself is beyond language and thought.

The Sanskrit meaning of Nirvana is "extinction, disappearance" (of the individual to the cosmos). In simple words, it means "quenching" or "blowing out," in the way that the flame of a lamp is blown out. When the oil of a lamp ends, the lamp extinguishes. Thus, when a person's desires, which are compared to the oil, come to an end, he/she attains Nirvana.

For those who want to further go deep into this subject, the "Nirvana Shatakam" (Atma Shatakam), a composition of ancient Indian supreme guru Adi Shankara (796 CE) depicts Nirvana as the disidentification of the manifested self and recognition of pure blissful consciousness as the ultimate end and reality.

Adi Shankara composed the Nirvana Shatakam, to address the ultimate self (in Sanskrit he gives the name "Shiva" to the self) as the highest reality. The essence of the composition is to tell that Shiva himself is everything, but still, he (the self) is nothing.

The meaning of Shiva is "embodiment of grace". The word "Shiva" means literally, "that which is not." Shiva according to Adi Shankara is pure consciousness whose nature is Sat-Chit-Ananda (Existence, Consciousness, Bliss absolute) or Brahman.

Nirvana Shatakam was sung just before his Nirvana, that's why the name Nirvana Shatakam. Shatakam means six verses.

It starts with this verse:

"Mano buddhi ahankara chittani naham

Na cha shrotravjihve na cha ghraana netre

Na cha vyoma bhumir na tejo na vayuhu

Chidananda rupah shivoham shivoham"

I am not mind, nor intellect, nor ego, nor the reflections of the inner self (chitta). I am not the five senses. I am beyond that. I am not the seven elements or the five sheaths. I am indeed, That eternal knowing and bliss, the auspicious (Śivam), love, and pure consciousness.

Those who are interested may begin by meditating and reflecting on these broader indications.

CHAPTER – 19

And Finally: Are You Enlightened?

"Have you ever heard about enlightenment?" he asked while running his fingers through his long beard.

"I am already enlightened" I replied with a serious face, hiding my laugh.

"What?" his shock was evident from his croaked voice. So, far he had an artificial softness and slowness in his voice. That act of being calm disappeared from his face. The real him was visible.

"I said I am enlightened" I repeated.

He gave me a blank stare. Then, touched the turban that he uses to cover his bald head. And nodded his head as if I have totally gone nuts.

"Do you have any problems with that?" I asked.

"No…no…but, you see…" again, the artificial tone came back to his voice: "Enlightenment is a very serious, big, deep thing…you don't understand…"

"Oh…come on…It is the simplest thing under the sun. You don't understand" I replied.

He nodded himself in disagreement. Only a close observation could detect the anger that splashed in his eyes. "See brother, you don't look like an enlightened person."

"Really? …then, please tell me, how an enlightened person should look like?"

"Hmm…your dress…"

"Oh…Is there a dress code for an enlightened person? Is it casual, party wear, or formal?"

"Are you serious or pulling my leg?" his eyes narrowed down while asking this question.

"I am very serious, Sir. I am an enlightened person, you know. But I didn't know that there was a dress code or uniform for enlightened people."

He didn't answer for a while. Sometime back, when I started talking to him during a trip to Bangalore on the train, he introduced himself as a high-grade assistant to a famous spiritual guru. He is among the privileged second-man-in-command. In due course, based upon his seniority and performance, he can even be a guru, he said. We both were sharing the same coupe. There were no other passengers in the coupe that had four berths.

"It's not like that, you won't understand…"

"You are a Guru-in-waiting. So, could you please explain to me, so that I will learn?" I asked.

"You should dress like a detached person…" he said.

"What do you mean by detached?"

"Aha…you don't even know about detachment…And are talking big-big things about enlightenment…." he laughed loudly as if he won an argument. Abruptly, he stopped his laugh and put on a serious face.

"Sir, what is detachment? And what is the dress code for enlightenment?" I asked again.

"Detaching from the worldly pleasure…detaching from the family bondage…the freedom comes from detachment…happiness comes from detachment…then we will lead to enlightenment… you still have family and want to enjoy worldly pleasures, right?"

"Of course, yes…worldly pleasures are important for me, but

without exploiting others…now you said, detachment, means freedom from bondage, right?"

"Yes."

"This means, your concept of freedom is limited to detachment. Your concept of happiness is limited to detachment…" I said. "But as far as I am concerned, freedom and happiness have no fixed borders…I am happy when I am attached. I am happy when I am detached too. Similarly, I am free in detachment and free in attachment too…"

"That's kutharka…" he said. (kutharka = malicious reasoning on the part of those who do not understand the real significance of the scriptural texts which are substantiated by logical reasoning)

"No Sir, it is vitharka…" (vitharka = has a meaning close to argumentative mode with reasoning, understanding but clarifying too) I said: "I have an open mind towards happiness and freedom. You have a conditioned mind, and you propagate that concept, I am not…now, please tell me about the dress code…"

"I mean…the dress should be like that of vairagyi's (detached man)…like saffron or white…"

"Like yours? Imported silk cloth stitched by branded tailors?" I tried to tease him.

"No…I didn't claim I am enlightened…" he snapped back… "And you are arrogantly saying that you are enlightened and wearing a flashy t-shirt and cargo jeans…Haha!"

I told him a story. While I was doing my graduation, I had a sickness of writing short stories and poetry. I have been selected as the best short story writer in the university. So, I was invited to attend a three-day "literature camp" in a remote forest resort camp. I traveled down there. There were three people in the front desk reception. Looking at me one of them asked: "What can we do for you?"

"I came here by invitation."

"Are you a sponsor or something?" the receptionist asked.

"No...I am a writer..."

All three of them gave me a strange look.

"You don't look like a writer"

I asked, "why?"

"No...most of the writers have a pattern of dressing. Pyjama, Kurta, Beard, and a cloth bag with long strap..."

"Some of them are smelly too..." one person cracked a joke.

"You are in T-shirt and jeans...there is no beard..." the other one said.

This is a popular misconception. A perception. We believe in that concept. Our minds wouldn't allow it to go wrong. If something goes against our long-standing perception, we will feel like dying by suffocation. Nobody wants to break such conditioning, even if we have chances.

He listened to this flashback incident carefully but didn't comment anything.

"I am enlightened...the only difference is, I didn't have a rigid concept of how an enlightened person should be. But you have a strong concept, one which I don't fit into. Is that my problem? " I said.

"You mean to say you are right and I am wrong?"

"No. I am saying, according to me, I am enlightened. And, I don't have to convince others that I am enlightened. But you will need to..."

"What do you mean by that?"

"I am not in the business of enlightenment. You are. Your service area is meditation. And your final product is enlightenment..." I said, "You have deep conditioning of how an enlightened man should look like...Even the shape of the beard should fit into that concept…and you people dress like drama artists to satisfy the public's wrong concept on enlightenment…you wear a uniform to show others that you are spiritual gurus…your dialogues and voice modulation are also scripted accordingly. And you make money out of it…"

"You are talking non-sense…" he got angry. He raised his voice.

I smiled at him: "See, I am not angry at you. I am enlightened…"

"You never get angry?"

"Of course, I do. I get angry. I have all emotions…I become happy. I feel sadness…."

"And you call yourself as an enlightened man…"

"Yes – I am normal. That's why I am enlightened. I seldom hide my emotions or feelings…I feel my feelings. I observe my emotions. I experience my life as is without pretension…hence I am enlightened…I am an ordinary person…I don't show any miracle…so I am enlightened…"

"So, you mean to say, the enlightenment is for all – for every Tom, Dick, and Harry in the street? You need many years of Sadhana. And you say, it is so easy?"

"Yes, coming to that, even you can be enlightened?"

"Even me?" he raised his eyebrows. His face again turned red.

"Just joking…seriously, you are already enlightened. You may not be aware of it. It is as if we are just closing our eyes and we are crying, "I can't see the light."

"Please continue, sir, very interesting," he said.

"All I can I say is: "Just open your eyes and you will see that the light is here." In fact, even "open your eyes" may seem to imply some doing. But I have to use some words, right? Enlightenment is very easy"

"Yes," he said. Now he is using his real voice. No artificial soft and slow tone." So, you have a different approach towards enlightenment and life?"

"No...I don't and can't claim anything..." I paused and winked at him and continued: "Except the claim that I am enlightened. I just say that I am a living person, an ordinary living person, almost happy with my life. My life too is with all the ditches around, with all the ups and downs of the roads around, struggles and miseries, comforts and enjoyments, with all the moments of change around, with all the pains and problems around..."

"So, when it comes to miseries, struggles, and hardships of life... how did you face it?"

"When I face miseries, I think of Ram, the Hindu God...Ram is the incarnation of the supreme cosmic entity Vishnu. Still, how much he did suffer in his life? Did he have a happy married life even for one year? No. Ravan has snatched his loving wife...He struggled his way out in the forest...Compared to Him, what have I faced in my life? Nothing...He is supreme lord for me. Still, he has suffered a lot. What does Life of Ram teach us? Life is full of miseries and struggles...and we should be happy that we got such a life. And that's the real happiness of life...knowing that life is all about struggles and sufferings, is really enlightening..."

"Hmm...you are talking sense; life is full of sound and misery signifying nothing..."

"Shakespeare..."

"Sorry, it was his quote... brother...yes, that's true...our problems are trivial..." He nodded to himself... "but how did you get really enlightened?"

I laughed out loud. "Just now, when you put on the switch in the compartment, tube-light lit and I got enlightened, thanks to you..."

"Brother, I seriously want to know. I know that you know many things and are just making fun of yourself...nobody has told me such things – they all talk high order philosophy of things... you talk normal things. Please answer my questions..."

"I don't have answers to your questions. You have to find your own answers. Nobody's answer is your answer. Everybody has to find his or her own answer because the problem created by life is a unique problem for you. And life is offering you the answer for that problem in that uniqueness. By just understanding this simple fact, I have begun my journey."

"Did you have a Guru?"

"Yes – thousands of gurus...Everything – every person I meet on the road, every experience I get, every incident of my life- everything is my Guru...- everybody I meet is my guru. Now you are my Guru."

"Me? What did you learn from me?"

"Even so-called higher spiritual people have deep conditioned, closed mind filled with concepts and perception..." I laughed. "No... Just joking..."

He passed it "You mean to say, you didn't have a guru that leads to enlightenment?"

"Nothing, nobody, or no teacher can help cause enlightenment to happen. Only you, repeat YOU, can do it..."

"Ok, if there was no Guru, how did you learn it?"

"Learn what?"

"How to get enlightened? Who taught you to meditate for enlightenment?"

"Brother...guru will teach his concepts of enlightenment...if that suits you, you can follow...I didn't have such guru – maybe I was not lucky enough to have one... The first thing I understood that knowledge at the information level won't transform me, and intellectual or logical understanding won't liberate me. Knowledge adds to my ego only. So, I began the process of unlearning. Then I found that my mind is deeply conditioned with wrong concepts and perceptions..."

"Then what happened?"

"BOOM...I am enlightened. The tube light lighted up above my head, Na? Thanks to the railways and you who put the switch on..."

"Sir...I am very curious...you are surprising me...please tell me, how did it happen? What was your experience?"

"You mean to ask, did I hear the bell ringing? Did I smell fragrance? Or did the heaven shower flowers? Come on yaar...those are all high melodrama and cinematic stuff..."

"No, I understand we had some concepts on enlightenment – probably wrong. But that's been taught to us for long period. But please, please tell me how did you experience it? What method or technique you used?"

"It happens naturally when the mind sees the limitations of all techniques, methods or guidelines..."

"Means?"

"Awakening is not even the effort to open your eyes. It is just waking up. It is as if you wake up from your sleep...awaken your consciousness by being aware, and you will find that the divinity is within you. And you are part of the being, you are totality...... and you're a perfect person with all your imperfections."

"Ok...I understand it on a conceptual level...But how did you reach there? How did you meditate? Some mantras?"

"Yes, I had a mantra...a big secret...don't tell anyone..."

"Ok."

I looked around and said: "It was: Mere sapnon ki rani kab aayegi tu, Aayi rut mastaani kab aayegi tu, Beeti jaaye zindagaani kab aayegi tu, chali aa, tu chali aa..."

"What?" he asked. I repeated.

He looked confused. Then he said: "I know that's an old Hindi song and you have made your point. There is no need for any mantras. I understand your point. But should we concentrate our minds to meditate? What's the process involved in your meditation? "

"This is another popular misconception…I can't afford to buy such a luxury process that you sell to clients to get enlightened."

"No…I just asked…"

"See brother, those who propagate meditation as "concentrating mind" believe that meditation is a voluntary process. We sit with closed eyes in a corner of the room (in places of worship/Ashrams) in a particular posture. Then we chant a mantra or sacred stanza from Holy Books or visualize the form of a god or goddess. We may then try to control our thoughts, this is what they say. This is what you normally call meditation, right?"

"Yes, what else?"

"Maybe true…I am not an authority to comment on this. I don't know. But as far as I am concerned, meditation is de-concentration. For me, it is not possible to concentrate on single object/thought for a long…"

"That's true. I also experienced. It is not possible to control the mind…"

"The gist of Bhagavad Gita, according to me, is a one-liner:- That which moves is mind. That doesn't move is GOD or cosmic"

"That's true. Beautiful… mind moves. But we talk about concentrating mind…"

"You don't walk the talk. I know. It is almost impossible to control your mind. Till this day, except in folklore or myth, nobody has ever done it – at least to my knowledge. Because you are using your own mind to control it… Mind control or concentration has absolutely nothing to do with meditation…"

"Ok."

"It is only temporary suppression of the mind. When the process – whatever process you use – ends the chaotic mind returns and things are back to normal...."

"So how are you meditating?"

"As I said, meditation is not a voluntary process at all. It cannot be invited. It is not the determined project of an isolated mind. It happens naturally when the mind turns within itself and is aware of its own movement. Meditation happens when we can see our desire and ego...when we see our own conditioning."

"So, what technique you used?"

"There is no technique to be in meditation. I told you -it happens naturally when the mind sees the limitations of all techniques. Being aware is the only way to make meditation happen. Observe and be aware. In awareness, there is no goal to be attained. Awareness is just the opposite of controlling or concentrating the mind. To be aware is to be with the moment, as it is."

"Then?"

"There is no struggle, as it is an effortless being in the NOW status. Observing self would lead to awareness. Awareness is also a silent announcement to the divinity that I am ready for the grace to happen. So, there is no process at all..."

"No process at all?"

"Nothing, but observing yourself. Observing thoughts – without judging or analyzing them – will lead you to awareness. As you observe you will know that you are not thoughts. Thoughts come, thoughts go, but you remain. As we observe, we would become aware of our thoughts, emotions, and actions...You will stop trusting your thoughts which are the product of your conditioning...You will become just a witness of your thoughts and you won't chase thoughts..."

"Then?"

"Nothing…you are enlightened…" I laughed again.

"Please tell me…"

"Sir, enlightenment is not a goal of meditation. Don't set any goals. Just be aware. By being aware, you will become aware of your life and love -and the divinity. You will take things as is. You won't misinterpret anything based on your conditioning"

"How will I know I am enlightened?" he seriously asked.

"You will stop asking such stupid questions" I laughed.

He didn't laugh. He thought for a while. Suddenly he asked: "Why don't you try to rectify the public about their wrong understanding on meditation and enlightenment? We could plan something."

"You are a spiritual businessman, so you think in terms of business…but I can't think like that…this is not my business"

"But as a free social service…you should reach public"

"Not my job. I am not an orator. I don't have any message to spread. I am happy with what I am…"

"But you have different ideas, concepts, perceptions, right? …"

"Number one -you don't verify what I said. You didn't experience if it is true. So, it is just another set of concepts or perception…you cannot generalize anything. Let others find their own concepts…"

"And number two?"

"Whatever I told you, are not my ideas. That belongs to my ancestors. They have given us everything free. I can't cheat them. I know successful modern spiritual industrialists have marketed such concepts in a colorful package as branded products and services…some of them have even patented it in America."

"I understand what you say, sir…spirituality is a big business now…but, you have a social commitment…commitments to your fellow human beings..."

"Yes. So, let's share and care the way we can. Everything happens with purpose. Those who are destined to share with me will come to me...I have met few people in my life and I have shared with them what I learned and cared for them...my social commitment is limited to that..."

"But ..."

"As I said, that is not my business. See, the popular concepts and perceptions about meditation and enlightenment were there in the deep psyche of the public for centuries together. People are deeply conditioned by such concepts. This conditioning is ego. Nobody wants to break the conditioning. The ego always needs security. Beating ego or de-conditioning is painful than death... they are comfortable with the concepts. And all they expect is to get an acknowledgment for their conditioning"

"Could be...I don't know...I don't understand..."

"I call it spirituality superstitions...Just like we live in a country with corrupt government administration or political system; most of the people are OK with that conditioning." I paused and continued: "So spiritual masters like you identify some basic concepts of meditation and enlightenment and decorate it, brand it, indifferent, value-added and colorful package. You don't want to change the public by de-conditioning them- you just want to exploit them. Result? The public is happy, you are happy – both are benefited. Who will challenge the system? Nobody. So, don't talk to me about social commitments. I, at least, don't exploit others..."

He closed his eyes. And remained in silence for few minutes.

"Hello...is there anybody here?" I patted in his turban and asked.

"Sir- that's awesome. You are earnest and honest in pursuing. I can't say how much did I benefit from talking to you. Now I am seriously feeling guilty of what I was doing now..."

"Why should you feel guilty? It is your job. I am a vegetarian. I am biased toward vegetarianism. But I am not a fanatic. If I insist everybody should be vegetarian, what will a butcher or a fisherman do? Everybody is doing his/her work. You are in the industry of spirituality. I am in the media. We both do our work and earn money to live…."

"Do you think so?" his voice was a bit shaky.

"Yes. I do. We feel guilty only when we do something wrong… you are a very good man. You have a good heart – otherwise, you won't realize so fast about your wrongdoing… you are a better man than me…I felt the vibes…You have no reason to feel guilty… try to come out of what you do, if it doesn't make you happy, that's all…what's the point in having guilt?"

I don't know. What happened next was very touchy. His eyes were filled with tears and he hugged me. Tears came to my eyes too. I was teasing the poor guy so far.

I said: "Forgive me brother…I was pulling your leg and making fun of you…I am sorry about it…I am not enlightened. I am just trying to be a funnyman… I am a truth seeker, that's all…I was trying to act smart with you to beat your ego…" I meant it.

"No sir…It is not like that. Today, I understood my flaws. I looked down upon people and I thought we were superior beings as we are "spiritualists". People come to us when they face difficulties in life. And we make money out of the situation…I understand that"

"That shows you are a very good human being…"

"There are thousands of enlightened people around me. Those who are enlightened won't show it. Those who are not will act as they are enlightened. And only those earnest seekers with divine grace could see or understand the enlightened people. You are truly enlightened. Thank you, Sir."

"You have got wrong ideas about me. I am not enlightened. I still have a lot of conditioning. I have not come out of all concepts... as I said, I am just a normal human being and want to remain like that...I don't want to be enlightened. My enlightenment is being with my loved ones. Let me live the life that comes to me. I am happy with the miseries and struggles in my life. I also have all tensions, stress, and problems in life. But I just love it" I said.

"No sir, I understood you properly. I know there will be a lot of people like you who don't want to convert everything into business..."

"Hmm. It looks like you are absolutely enlightened now. An overdose of enlightenment. But I am fed up with being enlightened. So, let's put off the light so that we can sleep..."

(End)

ABOUT THE AUTHOR

Udaylal Pai

Udaylal Pai has been a professional journalist specializing in business, finance, and technology for the last 30 years. He has worked with many Indian and international media. Apart from his profession, as an author, he has been writing articles, sharing his experience. Santana Dharma, Science, and Mind are his favorite subjects. Though he has been writing exclusively for his website, his articles have been widely re-published and re-posted all over the world with at least a million readerships.

BOOKS BY THIS AUTHOR

The Secret Of Krishna : Deciphering The Krishna Code

You Don't Eat A Lion Doesn't Mean Lion Won't Eat You: Why Do Bad Things Happen To Good People?

Why Am I A Hindu?: The Science Of Sanatan Dharma

Printed in Great Britain
by Amazon